WING CHUN FOR THE MODERN WARRIOR

JASON KOROL

ACKNOWLEDGMENTS

The strange thing about writing is that it's as private an activity as one can find in life and yet, surprisingly, also the most social. A writer would, after all, have nothing in the least to write about were it not for his/her relationships. Certainly, it's the same with me and, I should dare say, these encounters have been especially profitable in my particular case. Why? Well, because of the nature of the following people I'd like to thank. Each has played a pivotal role in my development as a Wing Chun man and I tell you soberly that I could not write this at all if it were not for their influences.

My brother, Michael, was the one who first introduced me to this glorious method of self-defense. Being eleven years my senior, he came home on break from college in the fall/winter of 1981. He wasn't home long before he began slapping me around in our shared bedroom in my parent's house in chilly upstate New York. He'd been learning the Alan Lee Wing Chun system and happily shared his discoveries with me. I've never ceased being a student of the method since that glorious beatdown.

But Michael wasn't just a mentor in the fighting arts. Being a photographer and artist, and a deeply philosophical thinker as well, I learned the ins and outs of Wing Chun from a mind that loved beauty and truth too. My early teenage years were, therefore, impacted greatly by his presence. I often labored through long, boring days at school until we could meet up again to practice chi-sao, talk about all the wonderful ideas of Kung-fu, life, and art. It was a magical time that I tried to transport to the school I have now.

My Sifu Tony Massengill, who I met in 2010, has been a tremendous and inestimable mentor, leader, and friend. I would go so far as to say that over the years he's become a brother to me. From the minute I walked into his school one August night in Virginia, I could tell that he was my kind of man – a man of ideas and action. Sifu Tony is that rarest of finds in the martial arts world: an instructor who honestly and fervently desires that his students surpass him. I remember one time when he remarked, matter-of-factly, that if at the end of his life he hasn't made students better than himself then he's actually weakened the system he was supposed to be teaching.

In the years before I met Sifu Tony – especially in the late 90's through 2010 – I had developed a rather allergic reaction to Wing Chun due to the politics and illogical traditionalism that seemed nearly ubiquitous. A few hours with him, though, restored that great love I first had for the art on that night back in New York as a 12 year-old. He is an instructor that pours out information and deep concepts at a breathtaking pace. And it's all backed up by solid performance skills and realism gained through a career in law-enforcement and public service. Clearly, unequivocally, this book isn't possible without his guidance, encouragement and support.

You can learn more about Sifu Tony at ipmanwingchun.com. He's also the author several books, most recently, Hard Target, which is an excellent primer on self-defense for the novice.

I would also be amiss if I didn't thank the tremendous and Godly people I have around me at Greenville Academy of Martial Arts – especially Aaron Bouchillon. Aaron began training with me in 2007, never having done JKD or Wing Chun. He has grown over the years to be a man of great skill and insight into these systems and I'm sure that after I've written my last book and thrown my final punch, I will have left the Wing Chun world a better place with him in it. His ideas and dedication have already helped our program grow. He is a true Christian gentleman, a man of deep and abiding honor, a trusted friend and ally, and the future of Academy JKD and Wing Chun.

The rest of our "cast" here in Greenville, SC is a blessing from God as well. They are all tremendous martial artists and people of great character. Devin Smith, Jazilyn Wiley, Randy Fang, Josh Seawright are all constant inspirations and delights for me to know. Also, the entire Compagna family has been a great blessing throughout the writing of this book. Their fellowship and support are deeply appreciated.

For more information about Academy Wing Chun, you're welcome to visit our website greenvilleacademy.com. Information about distance learning, seminars, private instruction, and contact info are all there.

Sifu Tony doing chi-sao in Foshan, China with Ip Chun, Grandmaster Ip Man's eldest son. Tony was there that day to have his book, *Mastering Wing Chun,* placed in the Ip Man museum. He co-authored the book with his Sifu, Samuel Kwok.

Sifu Tony with Ip Ching, Grandmaster Ip Man's youngest son.

Ip Ching, Sifu Tony and Samuel Kwok. Sigung Kwok is the only man to be a master instructor under both of Ip Man's sons.

Me with Sifu Tony at my school in 2013. This is one of my favorite photos.

1

A QUICK NOTE

This book is intended to serve as a foundational overview of the heart-and-soul of the Wing Chun system. I don't intend simply to show you how - but also *why*. In doing so, I would like to alert the reader to the abundant - and free - course material available on the Greenville Academy of Martial Arts YouTube page. Three separate videos on Wing Chun's first form, Sil Lim Tao, running well over an hour total, will provide you with a tremendous training aid. We shot those videos, frankly, with this book in mind. Obviously, video can do things a book can't and yet the same is true in reverse. That being the case, I think a book is better suited for a comprehensive overview of the fighting method's core principles. In saying that, it's critical to understand how important it is to get the big ideas right. The book, therefore, will focus primarily on those key concepts.

When properly understood, the Wing Chun student will have a strong foundation - both theoretically and structurally - upon which to build. In doing it this way - that is, systematically - I hope to present Wing Chun as the premier real-world self-defense system. To that end, I must, as a corollary, defend the system from internal misapprehensions and external critics. The internal errors arise from either not knowing the core principles or playing one principle over against another. External critics seize upon these lapses and write Wing Chun off as a valid self-defense science. To answer them, it's necessary to define the nature of real-world violence. In this manner, the book will serve as a sort of *apologetic* (a reasoned and logical defense) against critics and errors.

The first Youtube video in our Sil Lim Tao series will provide a helpful overview of these principles in action as you read the book. You can watch it at www.youtube.com. (For those with the print version of the book go to http://youtu.be/ZbWQ9Rz9XLs). My suggestion is to view the video when you come to chapter nine as that's where we begin to delve into that material in earnest.

The very first thing we'll do, however, is look at the direct application of Wing Chun in the most common self-defense scenarios. These examples are Wing Chun's heart and soul as the method's primary objective is to repel a sudden, violent attack. Sport application is not the goal of Wing Chun. Its primary and guiding purpose is for the deployment of logically consistent tactics and techniques to save your life in the event of an unavoidable attack. There are other benefits, of course, like improved fitness for example. Such things can also be said of dance or CrossFit, though, but they will be of no use to you if someone tries to kill or rape you. Brutal simplicity is the key because under pressure, complexity breaks down.

The second aspect of the book covers the ideas that buttress a combat martial art and the core principles of this self-defense system. All of this is interrelated - the action and the theory/philosophy. Living as we do in such an anti-intellectual age where we've been educated to think of ourselves as "practical" people (that is, opposed to theory) - although that's a theory itself, but more on that as we go), I hope to convince the reader that sound philosophy is eminently practical. Not just that, but for the self-defender, an accurate understanding of the issues at hand are essential. In all, it's a critical mistake to teach the physical actions of self-defense absent the ethical realities undergirding them. As we'll cover later, the martial artist isn't merely a "fighter", but a philosopher of the fist.

Thus, the goal of the book is two-fold: to show you what Wing Chun does and, importantly, why it does it. To leave out the latter opens the door to the deterioration of the former as all action is based on ideas. To give you Wing Chun, I must give you the mind as well as the body.

A good many people have written to me over the past year about our Wing Chun videos to say how much they appreciate the explanations of the forms. Many commented on how they'd been doing these strange movements and never knew why, nor how they were to be applied. This is quite flattering, of course. Nevertheless, it is as I suspected. Many people get into Wing Chun looking for a brilliant and simple self-defense system only to find it a bewildering and aimless labyrinth. Instead of finding a martial system where sound logic and practical application meet in a unique and efficient method, they find frustration.

This is because the actions aren't directed by sound philosophy and theory. By the end of the book, therefore, I hope that the reader will have a thorough understanding of not only what Wing Chun is but also what it isn't. In doing this, I understand that speaking of philosophy to people these days is a precarious bit of business. Marketing folks warn me all the time that it will turn people off. *Just give them the goods, man! Confuse em, and lose em*, they say. I have two things to say about that attitude.

First, that's insulting to the reader/student. Everyone can understand the basics of sound philosophy. In fact, everyone is a philosopher (of sorts) in that they must arrive at and act upon core beliefs about what are the chief aims of life. Philosophy isn't for ivory tower professors - it's for all of us. In fact, you're doing philosophy right now - you're sitting there and thinking about the nature of all this. Is it true? Is it important? How does this matter to me? These are all foundational questions that you already ask and answer all the time. The thing is, because the education system indoctrinates rather than teaches, most of us have been reared to think that philosophy isn't something we should worry about and/or it's beyond us.

That is, be sure, an infernal lie if ever there was one because you can see it right in the presupposition itself. Saying, "you don't need to worry about philosophy for your daily life" is actually stating a philosophy. That's the catch. I'm offering to the reader the power of their mind.

In this way, Wing Chun has been messed up for the same reason everything else is messed up: our minds are trained to think in "brute facts" (Cornelius Van Til)- disassociated bits of information connected to nothing. But all knowledge is interrelated and studying Wing Chun will give us a wonderful example of this. So, you can absolutely do philosophy - and do it where it counts! On the ground, in daily life.

Second, it's a lie to tell you that I can teach Wing Chun without giving you the ideas at the core of the system. Plus, the ethics those ideas are connected to and the metaphysic (ultimate nature of reality) that proper ethics rest upon must also be known. Just "giving someone the goods" turns Wing Chun into a commodity to be sold - like soap or shampoo. But a martial art isn't something you can buy, so to try that is disingenuous in the extreme. The individual is "buying" the book or the classes, of course, but the ideas and techniques must be integrated through thought and practice. In this way, a martial art instructor - or any teacher - should never pander to the audience. If my goal is to teach Wing Chun, therefore, I must logically express both the actions and ideas of the system in a way that inspires mastery in the student.

Lastly, this will give a robust understanding as to why Wing Chun isn't simply something like MMA or Krav Maga. Those are mechanical methods that speak nothing of the critical matters of personal ethics, sound theory, and force. While boasting of practical training, disciplines like the aforementioned leave out the greater questions that violence raises and teaches combat in a moral vacuum. On the other hand, I will forever and ardently insist that all martial artists be philosophers of the fist. Teaching violence in a vacuum because society has turned violent is a terrifying feedback loop. It's my belief that every person who raises their fist to learn to protect themselves needs the moral and logical principles undergirding their practice. That's my goal - to show the majesty and honor that comes from submitting to the disciplines that make us fearsome self-defenders but also loving and honorable men and women too. To have the first without the second is a contradiction in terms.

To give you an idea of the issues we'll cover, here's an outline of the material ahead.
    - Wing Chun in action (Chapter 3).
    - Wing Chun and self-defense overview (Chapter 4).
    - Why Wing Chun is the better alternative than sport-based methodology...safer in training and more applicable in application (Chapter 5).
    - The historical truth that proves the efficacy of Wing Chun (Chapter 6).
    - The philosophy of the warrior (Chapter 7).
    - Breakdown of the Wing Chun theory in Sil Lim Tao
    - The great danger of traditionalism in Wing Chun and how it turns a martial art into a religion (Chapter 18).

Lastly, to be clear, after the self-defense section in Chapter 3, the material is arranged through the use of essays addressing the topics at hand. Despite the progression of the material - toward the goal of integration and logical clarity - there will be a repetition of the main points. In particular, the reader will be reminded frequently of the reality of self-defense over against the mindset of competition. I'll make no apologies for this as I've found that this mistake is a critical and common one. As it goes, once the line is blurred between the two, one's self-defense is almost always infected by sport thinking. My reminders are like hand-sanitizing during flu season - protecting us from sport infection.

This format will also, I believe, assist the reader in going back over the material for future study. I assume that it's not as common to re-read a book in its entirety as much as it is to pick up an already read volume and glance over a pertinent chapter or two. It's with this in mind that the work is presented. In any event, toward the goal of mastery, repetition is always the key factor - whether with the body or mind.

2

GETTING STARTED

As you can see, I'm going to do something I normally don't do. I'm going to reverse the order of the material presented here. Normally, I'd give you the theoretical and philosophical foundation first and make sure our minds are on the same page and then move on to the things of the body. Yes, that's the way I'd normally do it. All practice is the practice of some theory and I wish to warn you that not knowing why something is true is more dangerous than not knowing the truth. The man who doesn't know the truth can always learn it, right? He can be told. But the fellow that has it but doesn't know *why* is likely to lose his confidence the moment there's a challenge (and truth is always challenged!). That's the danger.

Nevertheless, I'm going to get started with the application – the brutal simplicity of Wing Chun and then we'll cover the rest.

Wing Chun is built upon, and indeed is a martial extrapolation of the principle that the best defense is a good offense. But what is the best offense, you ask? A counter-attack. As you're going to see, whenever possible, we want to meet every attack with an attack of our own. That's the foundational goal of the entire system and I'm going to show you the basics of it straight away. After that we'll explain the system behind the brilliantly simple moves.

The attacks included are such assaults that we're likely to see in the so-called urban jungle. Since Wing Chun is a self-defense system, we aren't at all interested in using it for sport-combat. Sport fighting brings a number of variables to the table that differ from a sudden, violent encounter (and if it wasn't sudden, you should be sure, you missed an opportunity to leave the area before the fight started). These variables include safety equipment, rules, sure-footing and the like. But these differences, great as they are, really are small compared to the most profound difference between a violent altercation and voluntary sport-combat. That massive variance is "stalking." Everything that ensues in a sport-fighting engagement is colored by the fact that the combatants are stalking each other. Neither party is trying to escape, use obstacles/barriers, or, importantly, trying to make their way to a weapon. And these differences are no small thing, be sure. They change things so greatly that we need to be reminded on a daily basis because, if left to our own devices, our default setting is to try and "win" a fight, which is to say we approach self-defense the way we would a competition. This is dangerously obtuse thinking, however. Real-world, life-or-death violence is vastly different from competitive fighting in the same way that running out of a burning building is different than running a 5K race.

You don't need to win a fight – you need to not lose.

Don't ever, ever, ever forget this. Also, make sure you admit something right from the start too: it's your ego, your pride, that's your biggest enemy in just about everything you do in life. Lurking inside all of us is a prideful heart that wants to be special. We want to win. Sometimes this is good and sometimes it's not. For street-defense scenarios, it's liable to get us killed if we don't keep it in check (at least for men anyway).

Have you been cut-off while driving? That probably infuriated you. That person had no right to do it. It was insensitive. It was disrespectful. That's all true. But some of us get so angry that we struggle with road-rage. Think about it for a moment. It's fine to be a little angry that someone cut you off. That's not irrational at all. But to lose your temper is an example of too much pride. To get so enraged that you cuss and holler and scare your family, making them uncomfortable, perhaps ruining their day and eroding the confidence they have in you, is certainly not rational. Worse, some people even lash out at the other driver, follow them, gesture obscenely and so forth. In the most extreme cases, violence ensues.

To lose control of one's emotions to the point that they provoke a violent clash is exactly that which all martial artists should be trained not to do. But that's what unchecked pride does to us. So, let's be clear that we are studying a self-defense method – a means of protecting and maintaining our personal safety from a *sudden violent attack*. Pride has nothing whatsoever to do with this. If you're the type that's hyper-competitive, channel those passions into productive areas. You must. Take up BJJ or boxing or things like that – things that give you a productive outlet for your competitive energies. Or, get into another sport like basketball. Take up chess. Being competitive is fine so long as the competitor is working to channel the fire into productive areas of life that forces personal growth and, consequently, brings benefits to others. Fighting – the type we're talking about, doesn't do that. Violence never helps anyone although it is, sadly, sometimes necessary because we live in an evil world.

All that said, we're going to show the more likely type of assaults seen in street-fighting. We aren't going to assume that you're in a stalking match with another fellow. And then we're going to show the Wing Chun answers. You won't get one monolithic reply in any particular case. You'll get the simplest, most direct reply first and then we'll give you two variables in case the initial stop-hit (direct counter-attack) was either unsuccessful or you couldn't counter on that first action and a "defensive" action was needed first.

You'll notice that Wing Chun prefers the straight punch and straight kick for the majority of its counter-attacks. These, being very direct, are the foundation of our defense. The whole system is literally built around them. You might say that everything else in Wing Chun is there *in the event that the straight punch and kick don't work right away*. In this way, the footwork and all other actions support these basic tools and are not on par with them. If we keep this in mind and remember that Wing Chun rejects an egalitarian approach to its components, we'll do well.

The format is simple: counter-attack right away. If you can't do this, use footwork and counter-attack at the same time. If that's still not safe, use footwork and then counter-attack second. Also, we can parry/block and hit simultaneously. We'll explain the logic of this progression as we go.

3
SELF-DEFENSE

The stop-hit is always best - if you can do it. One thing to know about Wing Chun is that the rest of the system is there in case you can't use the stop-hit effectively.

Right Cross or Swing

Obviously, we'd prefer to beat the attacker to the punch. This takes practice, of course, but once you get the hang of using the Wing Chun punch properly, and it's truly straight, thrown with proper timing, the enemy will increase its power for you by virtue of running his face into it. That's one of the great benefits of the counter-punch – he helps you hit him harder.

A bare-knuckle punch is vastly superior to blows with a glove on. The damage of bone-to-bone contact shouldn't be underestimated and makes it highly unlikely that an enemy can "force" his way through the punch. Gloves - mufflers as the old boxers used to call them - protect reckless fighters. They'll have no such advantage against your bare fist. Hit first. Hit straight. Hit hard. Hit often.

The crazed right-hand punch is actually much harder to block than many martial artists like to admit, so don't be a martial snob. It's a powerful blow and its trajectory – angling in from the shoulder line – makes it difficult to defend with a block. The wider the blow, the easier it is to pick off, of course, but many street-fighters throw it in a semi-swimming motion, which will complicate many blocking actions. Add to this the fact that the puncher puts all his weight into the strike and it's much safer, if we can't hit him as the strike develops (stop-hit), to step to our right (away from the path of the blow) and counter-attack. You don't have to step far. *Many make the mistake of thinking that when we say "use footwork" that we mean jump around and move several feet. That's a straw-man mischaracterization of what we mean by footwork, however.* By sliding your right foot 6-12 inches to your right, and then shuffling your left foot after it the same distance, you will have achieved a safe position. Not only that, you will have a strong angle to counter-punch from as well.

Because of the overwhelming momentum the attacker uses with his right-hand punch, if it misses you, he's often off-balance. A great tactic to use at this point, provided you moved out of its path, is a push. This will open him up for a follow-up kick, throw him into something, off of something (like down a flight of stairs, for example) and/or make your escape possible. *In some cases, a good push is actually better than a strike.*

If the punch is wide enough, you can block/hit simultaneously. Depending on the circumstances, this can be riskier than hitting/moving because you're receiving the enemy's momentum. More still, by staying in the hot-zone you're vulnerable to follow-up strikes (or grabs/takedowns) that are harder to achieve if you had moved off the initial angle. A good plan is never to be where he thought you were going to be. No tough guy is so tough that he can do the impossible, which is to hit a target that he can't reach. And a moving target is always harder to hit than one that stands still. These two truths form the nucleus of smart self-defense. That said, using a block is sometimes needed and can be very effective when combined with a counter-punch. One must avoid the temptation of "playing catcher" and over-relying on blocking actions. Wing Chun abounds with cool and unique hand actions that students love to perform. I get it. They rock. My Sifu, Tony Massengill, once called *chi-sao* the crack of Wing Chun. What he meant is that it's so unique that students become transfixed, focus too much time on it, and forget that it's merely a drill. So, be forewarned. The material you see here first is absolutely, unequivocally the most important material for fighting. Don't stand still and duke it out. Move and fire.

On a side note, one we must consider, is the contention made by some Wing Chun people, that moving for defense is anti-Wing Chun. They say it's better to crash in and take the other guy's position and then finish him. This critique is flawed for two primary reasons.

Sometimes the attacker is able to line his shot up as is the case here. You can see that the angle Josh has is quite good and it's very hard to stop-hit or parry/block the attack.
This is why it's essential to be prepared to move. A moving target is always harder to hit than one that stays in the pocket.

Aaron side-stepped with great speed to avoid Josh's attack. Don't underestimate how much practice it takes to move like this under fire without losing your balance. You should also note the fact that Aaron didn't move too far either. He moved off line and is now prepared to take advantage of Josh's miss.

A push is a great tactic - especially in this case since after his miss, the weakness in Josh's position wasn't necessarily an open target as much as it was his balance. Aaron quickly moves in and catches Josh's center-of-gravity.

Self-Defense | 17

Notice how Aaron uses expert form - elbows in and weight balanced - as he executes the push. It's natural to lean with a push but the Wing Chun system teaches to use perfect balance in all things. This would allow Aaron to pursue Josh after the push or turn and run - or even turn to face another enemy.

A good push can throw your enemy - especially when he's already off-balance - a considerable distance. More still, it can allow you to throw him into things, over obstacles and even into another opponent. In this photo, Aaron is perfectly set up to wallop Josh with a heavy kick, escape, or pull a weapon if he has legal and moral right to one.

First, the critic has confused simplicity with over-simplification. There are several factors that can render such an aggressive counter-attack too dangerous. If, for example, the enemy is faster than you are, or larger, then evasion will be the first order of business. If "proper" Wing Chun meant never doing anything but crashing into the other guy with your own attack, then why is lateral and angling footwork even taught in the system? Clearly, the misconception is with those that are hyper-aggressive.

Second, the champions of such arguments are almost always large, strong men who have never had the experience of being overpowered by an enemy or training partner. True, if you are markedly larger and stronger than your enemy, you can be much more aggressive. The same tactic, however, can't be safely applied by a woman or smaller man who could be giving up several inches of height and maybe 100 pounds of weight.

One other thing to consider on this issue is that some proponents of "crashing into the attack" are merely confused about the efficacy of the stop-hit. Clearly, the stop-hit – or *jeet da* – being the simplest response, is the best. But, as we've covered, a variety of factors can render the simplest counter unworkable. In such an event the answer is to move and fire – a tactic that Wing Chun is a unique set-up for – or parry/block and fire. This is the utilization of the simultaneous attack and defense principle. In all, though, it's important to understand that no one tactic will answer every variable so Wing Chun provides for us the needed diversity of tactics while – so critically – avoiding over-complication.

Left hook

A long, looping left hook can be picked off with a good parry. If you moved out of the way of an initial right hand swing and the enemy follows up with the left, the parry-hit works superbly.

Most people are right handed, so you'll see more attacks from that hand than the left. In fact, I've seen many fights where both combatants threw dozens of strikes at each other but not one of them with the left hand. But, of course, it's fool-hardy to count on that. You very well may run into a left-handed puncher. In this case, we simply reverse the order. If the stop-punch doesn't work, we would need to move to our left (or back) to vacate the hot-zone. As always, using proper footwork is essential because it moves our ready-position/structure, which means we're able to instantly strike no matter where we are. This is the key skill in all of fighting.

Self-Defense | 21

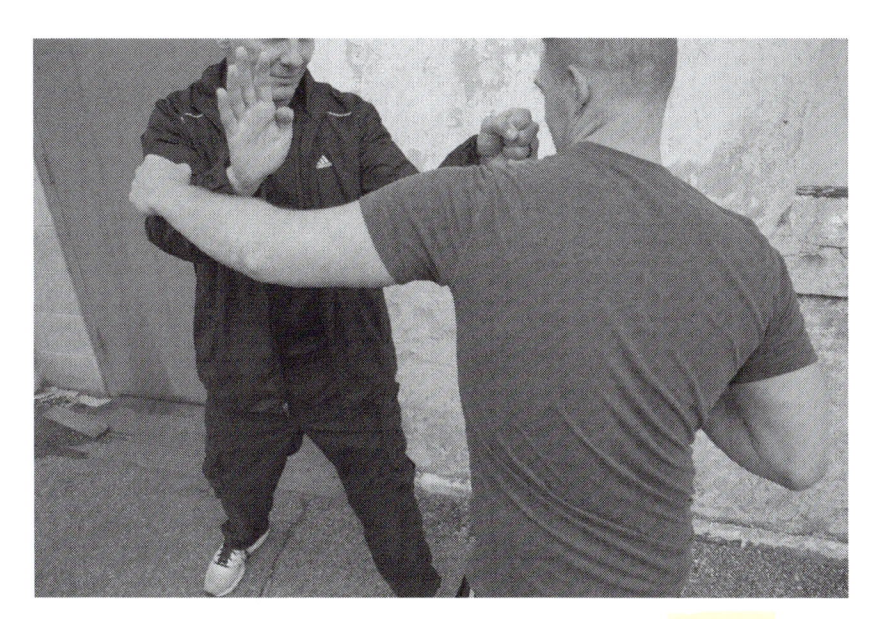

The parry can be used to help support a stop-hit and/or counter-attack. In every phase of fighting, your hands must be ready to pick off incoming strikes. In this way, the stop-hit, counter-attack, footwork and parry are all interconnected. Different scenarios might make one (perhaps the parry) more likely than another. The skill is in developing the fluidity and timing to instantly adapt to the situation at hand.

In this case, Sifu Jason used footwork to make the swing miss, which caused the attacker to over-extend. With the enemy at a disadvantage, a counter-attack is very safe and powerful.

The rush

Though not as common as a swinging attack, a large assailant can sometimes try and plow right into you, knocking you backwards and/or over. Then they'll proceed to pound on you. In this event, since our primary line of counter-attack is jammed, footwork and pivoting are essential. You can use a heavy leg kick as a stop-hit, but this is dangerous if your counter isn't sufficient to stop the attack as now you'll be off-balance. You should always judge your use of techniques with this in mind: if the action doesn't work, will I be in a worse position? This is why moving is superior to standing your ground – you don't have to be perfect. If your tactics are all-or-nothing you may very well end up with nothing. It's the red-light principle. All of us have run a red-light in our time. But it's certainly not something you should make a habit of doing because one of these days things could go very, very badly.

If the opponent is rushing you, move laterally or in a semi-circle. Only move as much as you need to and be ready to counter-attack instantly if/when there's an opening. A rushing attack is often used by someone quite a bit larger than the intended victim, which is another reason why it's smart to move out of the way and not try and rely on a stop-hit. After a successful side-step, though, you can always use a stop-hit as the attacker turns. Doing it that way diminishes the risk of getting caught in the storm.

The tie-up

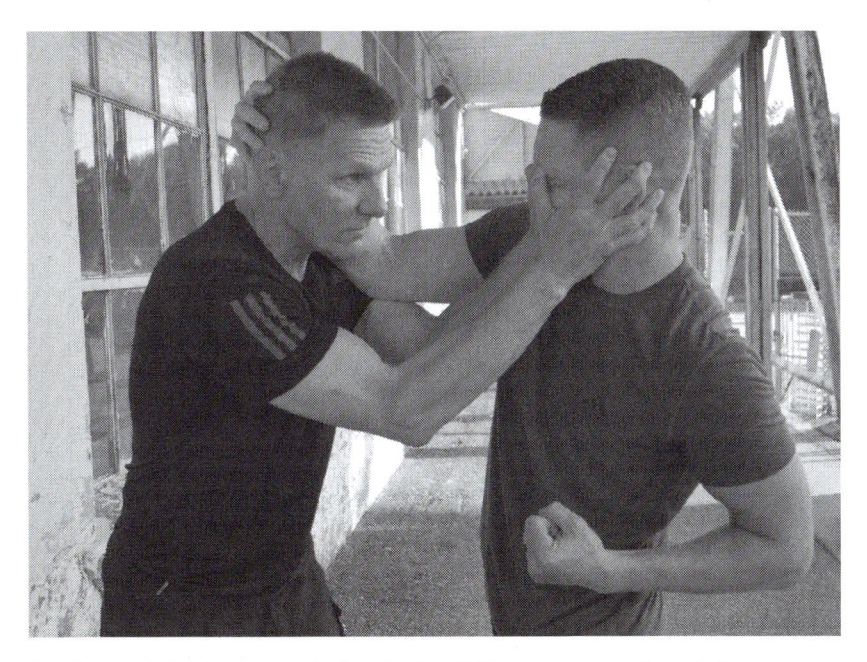

A serious omission in most methods today is in failing to protect and attack the most vulnerable parts of the body. If someone attempts to tie you up as in this photo, a two-handed eye attack - based on the fook-sau - is a tremendous tool.

Generally, a tie-up in a streetlight is a precursor to grappling. This is an extraordinarily dangerous situation for the self-defender because being on the ground with an opponent on top of you can very easily be deadly. Since this is the case, the Wing Chun fighter's close-range game is assiduously designed to fight off throws by keeping your guard in at all times. This creates a "fence" and makes it difficult for the aggressor to gain control unless he reaches around your fence for a handle.

In this event, the enemy leaves his middle open - thus exposing the most vulnerable parts of his body. There's a reason that a dog doesn't roll over and expose his belly unless he trusts you. In this case, you see the brutal wisdom of Wing Chun on full display. Wing Chun isn't a sport and if we take these tactics out of the equation, we no longer have Wing Chun. It's like a gun with no bullets. You have the appearance of a formidable weapon, but without ammo, your gun is really just an expensive brick. It's the same here. If we eschew these tactics, Wing Chun is impotent.

The proper eye-gouge must be a fast, violent and digging action. Hesitance and mercy will nullify the effectiveness of this valuable in-fighting weapon.

Self-Defense | 25

You'll notice the unique structure to these counter-attacks, which are specific to Wing Chun. No other system, to my knowledge, methodically trains you to attack and, importantly, defend these targets. In this way, Wing Chun is an art and science of dirty-fighting.

It's certainly understandable that these attacks might make you think twice. I must point out - because it's necessary to be unambiguous in this regard – that you're in a life-or-death struggle. Wing Chun isn't a game. If you're looking for a fighting method that will make you look cool but don't want to admit that to yourself, this section is the acid-test. If you end up thinking that you couldn't bring yourself to do these things in a fight, then you misapprehend the issue at hand.

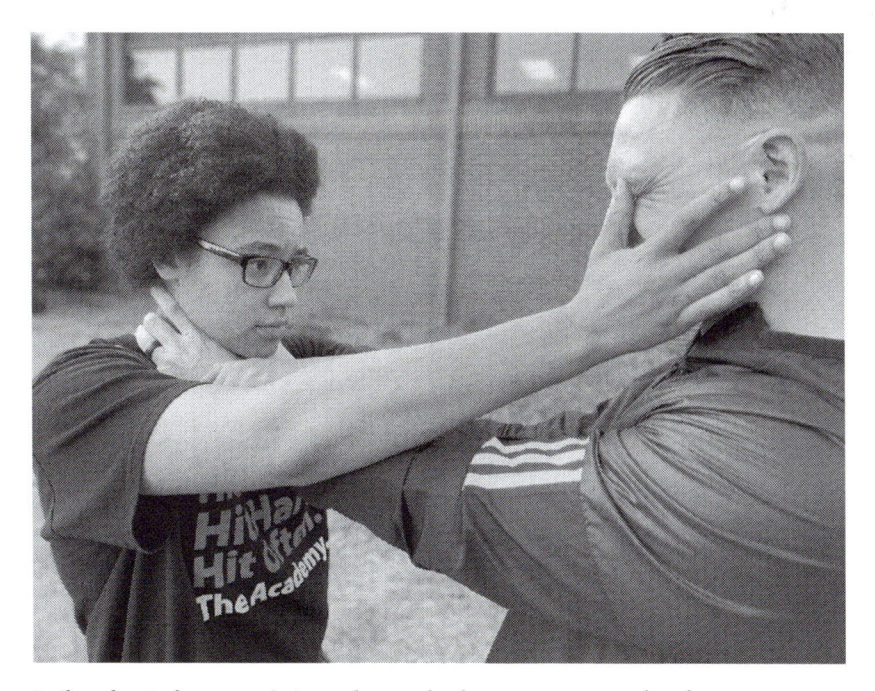

Jazilyn, despite her enemy's size and strength advantage, can neutralize the attack with the double eye-gouge. There is literally no reason for the Wing Chun defender to consider ANY other counter to in-fighting than disciplined attacks on soft targets.

A few years back we did a video on eye-gouges for our YouTube channel. A viewer commented that he could never do that to an opponent. One supposes that he considered such things barbarous and uncivilized. This simply exposed the erroneous presuppositions he had about violence. Violence is about survival. It isn't, as we've covered but need to repeat, about personal dominance unless we're the evil person rather than the defender. None of us should ever want to see a boxer or MMA fighter use these tactics in a match. That's the vile and reprehensible stuff of the Roman Empire – cheering as slaves killed and maimed each other for entertainment. No. We're talking about a true, honest-to-goodness fight for our lives. Anything less isn't worth fighting over, right?

If a confrontation goes to close-quarter contact, you're in an extraordinarily dangerous situation. Every part of your body is a target that's easily accessible and, for that matter, every part of your body is a weapon too. This being the case, speed and economy of motion are of the essence. The Wing Chun attacks at this range target the weakest links in the human armor. Never forget this. Once in "contact range" with the enemy the goal is to both attack his weakest targets while simultaneously defending your own. And this, ladies and gentlemen, is where the genius of Wing Chun is on full display.

We can easily deduce which targets are vulnerable. That doesn't take much analysis. The throat, eyes and groin are readily apparent. There are also attacks to the neck and jaw too. But which one of these should be primary? That's a question we should prefer to have settled before a confrontation. Leaving things to chance is an easy way to prepare for failure.

Well, the Wing Chun theory, presented in the Sil Lim Tao form that you'll get acquainted with later, gives us the idea of simultaneously attacking the enemy's weakest target *and* their center of mass. In other words, Wing Chun, as a matter of first principle, trains us to take the weak link and balance of the opponent simultaneously while also keeping ourselves as safe as possible.

So, what is this exactly?

The throat.

A driving strike to the throat with the right form/structure and footwork is the preferred counter-attack to any close-range engagement. The windpipe is a larger target than the eyes, easier to get at without compromising your balance (as is the case often with groin attacks) and uniquely available for follow-through measures.

All of Wing Chun is set-up for this attack.

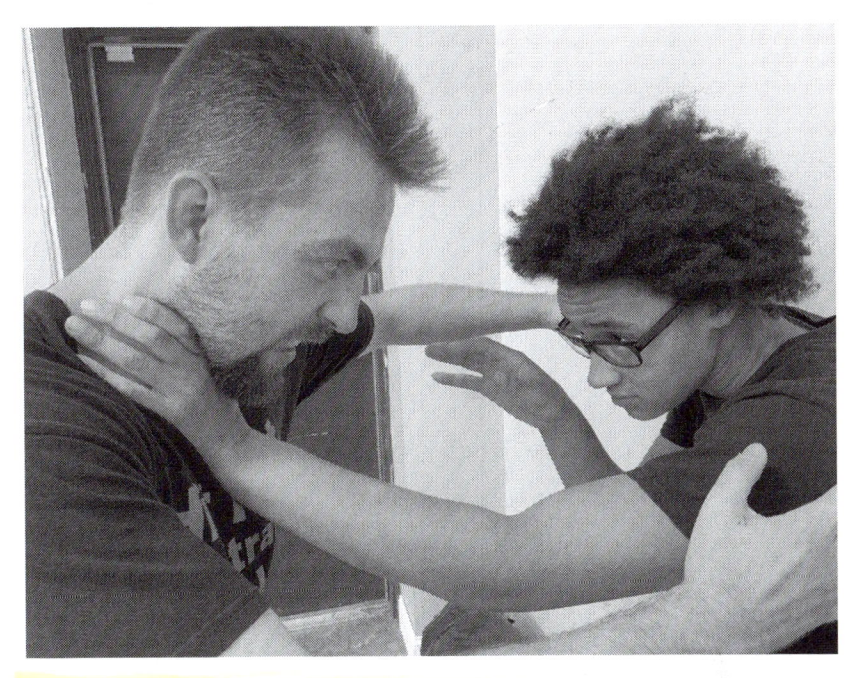

The throat strike is to in-fighting what the basic punch is to long-range combat. Used effectively, it can instantly end any confrontation.

One could safely say that boxing is a punching method and BJJ is a grappling method. To take these things away from the respective systems is to effectively render them useless, much like taking the engine out of a car. The seats are still in the car and one supposes they could go and sit in them but that's not the purpose of the automobile. Your living room is a better place to sit with friends. You sit in a car to go places. It's the same with Wing Chun too – it has a core component that, if denied, renders it useless and this is it. Up until this point you may have thought that the counter-attacks are interesting but that you could just as well use Muay Thai or Krav Maga.

This is where the brilliant uniqueness of Wing Chun manifests itself in fullness.

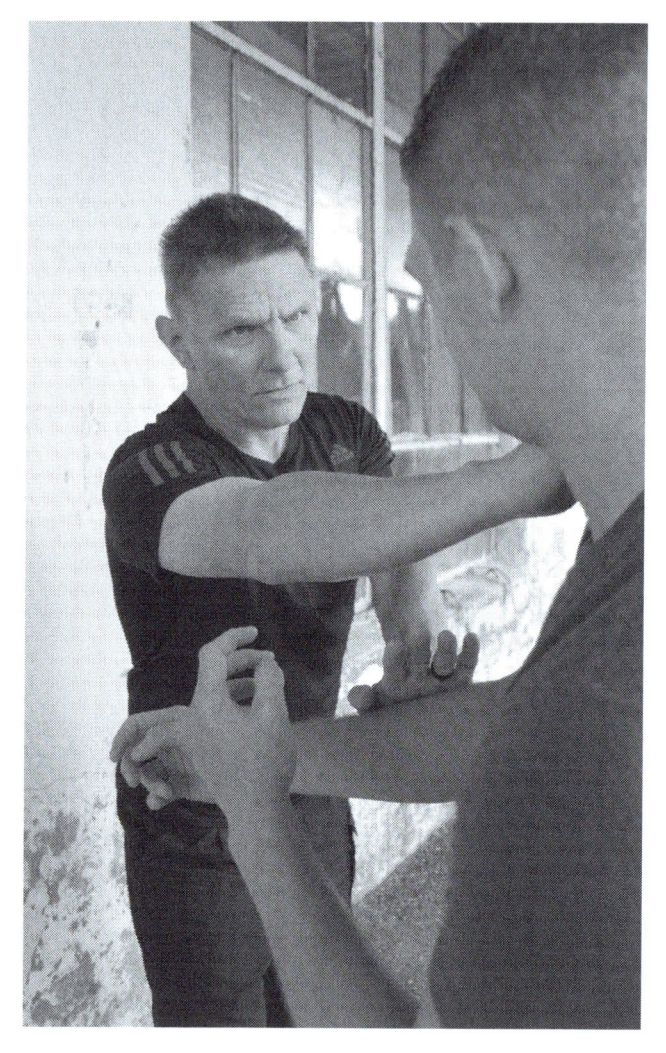

The neck strike is a chop and while not as efficacious as the throat strike, can still change matters quickly - even causing a KO due to a loss of blood/oxygen to the brain traveling through the carotid arteries.

Wing Chun gives you a non-contradictory method of overwhelming the enemy's weakest target – their throat.

Self-Defense | 29

Eschew this either directly or indirectly (by adding too much fluff and other strikes in a vacuous and misguided attempt to have variety) and you have extirpated the soul of the system. A good many Wing Chun exponents have lost sight of this brutal truth. That's regrettably true. They've done this because of two errors that you want to be vigilant against.

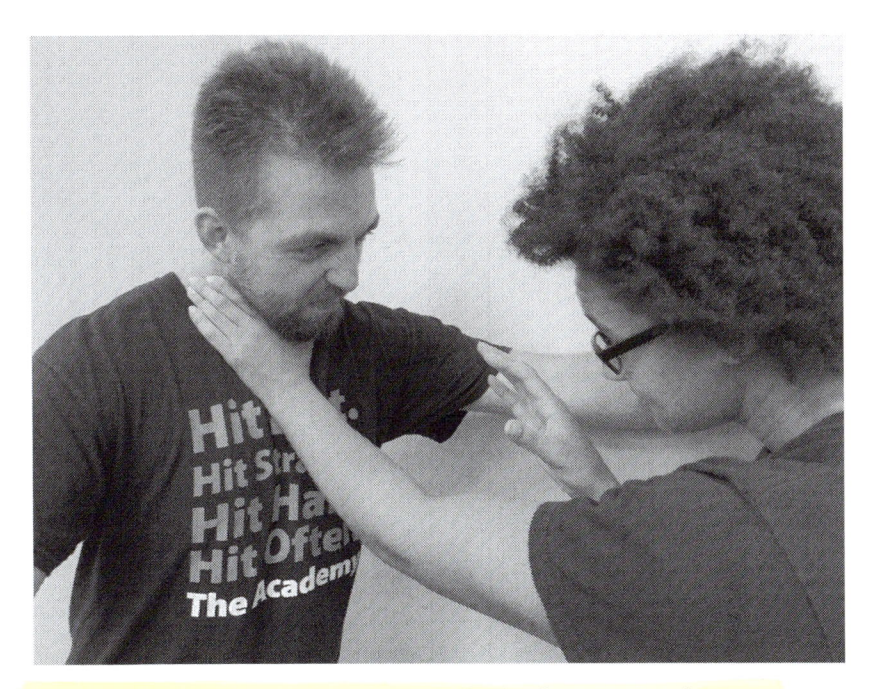

The proper throat strike is a snappy, driving push. The elbow must stay down to facilitate the driving power of the blow and to defend your center-mass at the same time. With the proper structure behind it, an aggressive foe will dash himself to pieces on this technique.

First, they refuse to see Wing Chun as a martial art – that is, warlike. They wish to domesticate it. It's like they get a lion and then pull its teeth and claws and treat it like a kitty. In this case, Wing Chun becomes inferior to other methods because they (methods like kickboxing and MMA, for example) are better at sport-based combat. Wing Chun is not meant to be a pretty weapon, but an effective one. Wing Chun is a *Glock*.

Next, the simplicity of it all bothers people, so they add stuff to it.

We make the error of thinking that having dozens of options means we're better off than if we only have one or two. But this is like thinking you have the advantage over the enemy because you have brass-knuckles, a hammer, steel-toed shoes, and a rock when your enemy has a gun. Yes, you have more tools but his, at the right range, renders yours useless.

The brutal math of Wing Chun in close-range combat is to take his throat. Other things come into play only when/if this becomes temporarily impossible.

Using the bui-jee to attack the eyes and throat at long range is certainly a good tactic too. It's harder to be accurate and powerful enough from a distance, however, so extra practice is necessary.

At a distance, these types of attacks are difficult to score, which is why the basic punch and kick are your workhorse. But once you're in-close against a grappler or in-fighter, the right form and structure will give you almost immediate access to the throat/neck of the enemy for the simple reason that no other systems bother to defend these areas. They just don't. That's why Bruce Lee called boxing "over-daring". Most BJJ fighters I know say that the best self-defense technique they know is the choke. For the most part, they're right. The Wing Chun version of that is the throat attack.

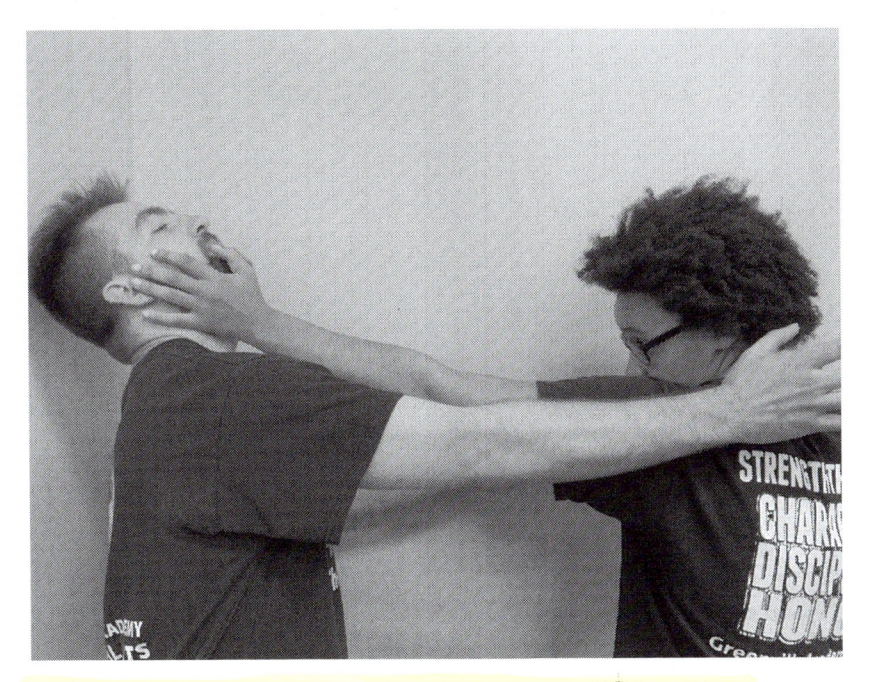

Striking the jaw is another valuable tool that Wing Chun provides. The side-palm - a fast, driving blow - is quite effective and leaves the enemy vulnerable to follow-up blows to the throat and neck. Grapplers are especially vulnerable to this blow.

Takedown defense

The Wing Chun fighter doesn't want to go to the ground. This doesn't mean, however, that we are to ignore grappling and hope for the best. There is middle ground between the positions of learning a grappling method and ignoring the very real threat. That middle ground is takedown defense.

A takedown attempt is a real danger in today's world. The first step to sound grappling defense is in staying alert and not getting over-extended. This is another reason why counter-attacks are preferred because there's less chance of overrunning your attack and getting caught in a double-leg.

In this case, with one leg forward, Josh starts an attempt at a single-leg takedown. By being alert to this danger, Aaron is ready and isn't off balance. Since the target is his leg, he begins to step backwards with it while also keeping a strong defensive position in case Josh changes tactics and starts swinging instead.

As Josh's shoulders reach Aaron's line of defense, Aaron swings his leg back and sends his "gum-sao" - or pressing/pinning hand downward. This dual action both hinders Josh's forward momentum and gets Aaron's leg out of harm's way. Notice Aaron's balance and preparedness for a follow-up.

As Aaron completes his single-leg shot block, he is very well positioned to counter-attack due to Josh's loss of balance. But even still, Aaron is ready in case Josh changes directions and shoots for the other leg. ==Balance is key!==

The blocking hand is usually the hand on the same side being attacked. This is a flexible rule because the Wing Chun system is ambidextrous and though we may have a leg forward, we don't necessarily have a side forward.

Grappling defense on the street differs from wrestling in the gym where there are mats. On asphalt or cement, the more commonly taught takedowns are rather injurious to the grappler due to the fact that they rely on the mats to protect them from the elements. For this reason, it's more common to see "dives" as with Josh than this attempt.

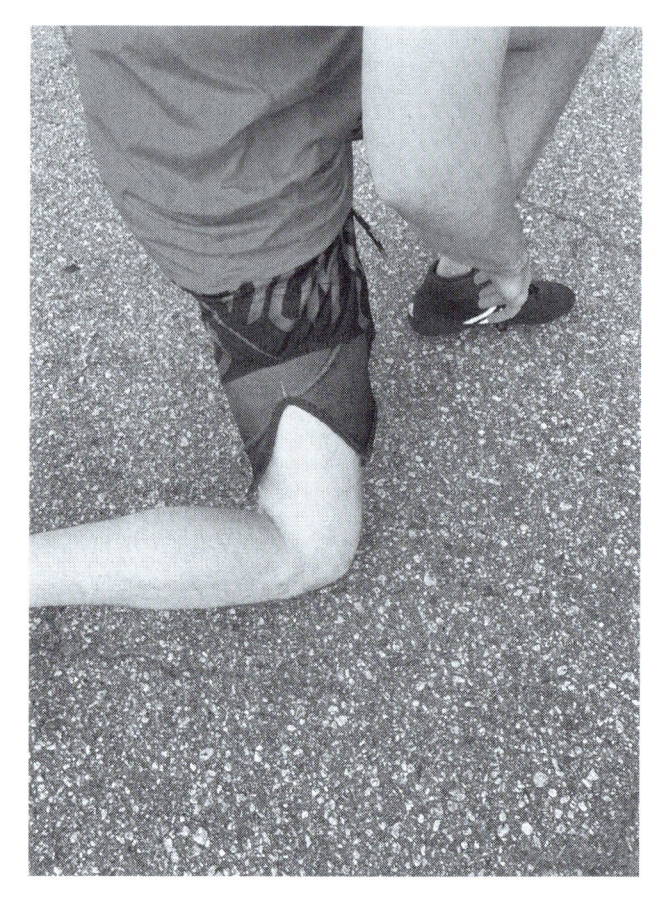

If the grappler lands on his patella it's very likely that he'll be seriously injured by the ground.

Secondary attack from another opponent

There is simply no way to account in a book for every type of scenario but suffice it to say that in today's world, any altercation you're in is a potential multiple opponent fight. I've seen cases where a fight starts and someone, who doesn't even know the combatants, takes a swing at one of the fighters just because he can. That's crazy, I know, but it's the world we live in.

Self-Defense | 39

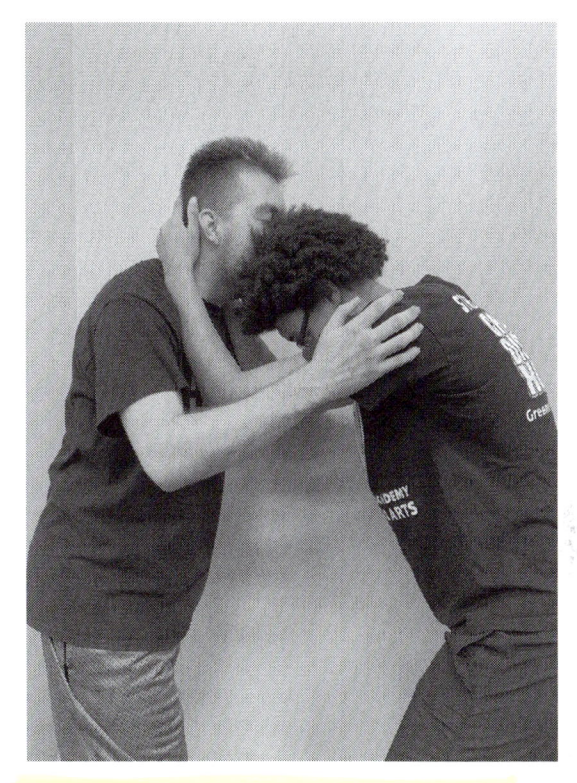

A head-butt is sometimes in order. Use it only to the foe's face and only with the top of your head. Never butt with your forehead. It should be deployed in a quick, short fashion - like a jab. Don't smash with your head as the distance is short and too much can go wrong. Used judiciously, the head-butt is a frightening tool.

For that reason, it's advised that you are always aware of this potential danger and, therefore, keep your head on a swivel. A great mistake in martial art training is the concentrated focus in drills (especially sparring) on only one opponent. For our purposes, we should always be checking our six (behind us) and our flanks. It's common that by just being aware of the threat that it's enough to discourage aggression from a would-be assailant. He's looking for a sucker-punch, after all, so don't be a sucker.

4

FIREARMS, WING CHUN & SELF-DEFENSE

A common error in America, where gun ownership is common, is for the gun owner to eschew hand-to-hand knowledge in favor of the gun. This makes it almost certain, however, that any self-defense altercation the gun-owner is involved with will include deadly force. Not every scenario requires shooting someone, though. Nor can you always access your firearm and/or safely deploy it given the environmental considerations. A true martial artist, which is what a gun owner really is whether he wants to admit it or not, should absolutely know how defend himself with his own body.

Unfortunately, a good many gun-owners don't avail themselves of a hand-to-hand system. Indeed, in many conversations over the years, I've seen a familiar pattern. Many of these individuals have done their training through military and/or police instruction and simply haven't been able to make up their mind about a hand-to-hand system. This is usually because there are so many competing theories concerning how best to protect yourself with an unarmed combat system. Without fail, such persons are always practical men and women who can't fathom themselves jumping around in some dojo, wearing expensive pajamas and learning convoluted katas. It all looks like a sad, pathetic game of make believe to them.

Likewise, they see the grappling-based MMA type-systems and feel a wee bit uneasy about all that ground fighting. Isn't being on pavement, a guy on top of you, perhaps wrestling for your weapon, a bad idea?

Yes, it is. Trust your instincts.

Other folks who have no military or law-enforcement background, see martial art training as unrelated to the goal they have, which is self-defense. They're actually right. Interested only in sudden, violent encounter defense, these types of men and women look at most martial art training and see it as something divorced from the goal they have in mind. To this, again, I declare that for the most part they're right. It's just that the Wing Chun here is the hand-to-hand system they need to compliment their firearm training.

In Wing Chun we aren't burdened by the insanities (and over-the-top commercialism) of modern American martial art training. What we get, on the other hand, is a brilliantly simple – yet comprehensive – system of close-range unarmed combat that actually compliments the tactics and principles we already know from firearm training. In fact, I'd go so far as to say that every gun owner *should know* Wing Chun. Tony Massengill actually teaches handgun application based on Wing Chun and the CAR (Central Axis Relock) system. In his view, they are flip sides of the same self-defense coin. One without the other is incomplete.

There are objections to this from within the martial art and Wing Chun world, of course. This hesitancy exists, one assumes, because of the growing pacification of the civilian population. There is, in many leftist circles of thought, more suspicion of free men and women owning firearms than there is of criminals. This is an alarming development and a symptom of creeping statism to which we must remind the reader that a free man or woman has both the natural right and duty to defend themselves. In a society where criminals don't fear self-defenders, there is more violence, not less.

Also, all martial arts from antiquity have included weapons training. I repeat: all warriors carried weapons and trained in their use. Only slaves, servants, and the oppressed were forbidden from carrying tools of defense. They couldn't, be sure, because they were slaves, not free. Therefore, a modern martial artist should know how to handle modern weapons. Training in the use of the sword is fine. Knowledge of Wing Chun's *baat jam do* form (eight slash knives) is great - but not at the expense of handguns and shotguns.

So, in all, since Wing Chun is a true system of defense against real-world violence, there is no contradiction between it and firearm training. They are, rather, extensions and applications of the same logical principles.

With that said, we'll now shift our focus to the principles and tactics of the system. We'll focus primarily on application principles and less on technical details for the simple reason that a technical detail is true or false only so far as it's applicable in reality. Much trouble can be avoided in our martial studies when we keep this in mind. Application against a real living threat is always paramount. Martial arts in general, and Wing Chun in particular, has been grievously guilty over the years of focusing too much attention upon technique and very little on performance. They bemoan the sloppiness of a boxer or MMA fighter from the safety of their dojo where everything is rehearsed. We'll do no such thing here. In fact, we'll focus on exactly why Wing Chun is a true self-protection science for real world combat and not – repeat not! – a museum piece passed down through the ages for preservation.

To do this, we're going to take a deep look at the system's first form, Sil Lim Tao. And not only will we look at the form, but for this volume, we're going to focus extensively on the form's first four sections. Crazy, huh?

Now, I can hear you saying, *"Are you kidding? I'm looking for something practical and you're giving me a stinking form!?"* Well, yes and no. You see, the Sil Lim Tao (SLT) form is unique in that it isn't a series of imaginary fighting scenarios. Instead, it's an alphabet of foundation concepts and tools. It presents the core technical details, yes...but more importantly, it also delivers the system's brilliant and non-contradictory application philosophy as well. Indeed, if you understand the core principles of the SLT form's first four sections, everything else in the system – every drill and form to follow – will make sense. But if these core concepts are ignored, or misunderstood, then much of what follows will lose context and errors will abound.

We repeat: all mistakes in Wing Chun find their provenance in either an ignorance of the form's first four sections and/or in playing one aspect over against another. As you'll see, these four sections are all interrelated and have an indivisible relationship with one another.

Let's use firearm training as a reference. Any individual that's taken a gun course has learned the following: *assume it's loaded, don't point it at anything you don't intend to shoot, keep your finger off the bang-switch until you've decided to shoot, and know what's beyond your target.* These safety rules are designed to keep us from doing the unthinkable: shooting someone by accident. These rules are so ingrained in responsible gun owners that they don't believe in such a thing as an "accidental discharge" of the firearm. There's only *negligent* discharge of the weapon because if the aforementioned rules are followed rigorously, no one gets shot that shouldn't be shot (like a bad guy, or a lawyer...but I repeat myself).

We can see the first four sections of the SLT form in much the same way except this also goes into application detail as well. So, in a way, when the Wing Chun fighter is good, he's good because he's so developed these critical principles that their application is second nature. There is integration in everything he/she does.

We must remember that doing something that's simple – under the intense pressure of a violent assault – will not be easy. Indeed, *simple doesn't mean easy*. The *Navy Seals* are rightly considered elite soldiers. But complexity bias comes in when we think of such warriors. The big reason they're elite is because they are so good at the basics. In fact, in any field we turn to, it's the basics that matter. Proper execution of the basics under pressure is the goal. Proper execution of so-called advanced and convoluted training in the safety of a school is antithetical to real martial art.

In the field of firearms and knives, students often make this mistake – they add complexity to their training, thinking that the simple things are beneath them. So, they add all manner of gadgets to their guns and do super-complicated knife drills. It's all dangerously stupid nonsense. When seconds count, it's the basics that matter and that's what we have to train for with any weapon - including our own body.

Of course, with a firearm, you're given a weapon fashioned by the hands of another; in Wing Chun, you're becoming a weapon. Tony Massengill (whom I quote rather liberally throughout this book... sometimes even giving him credit), refers to the SLT form as *"building the weapon."* And that's exactly what's happening.

Lastly, to help you get your head around all this, remember that Wing Chun consists of five parts. The forms come first because they teach and detail the principles and tools (techniques) in the system. These must be learned, understood and trained in order for the student to use Wing Chun. Any attempt to do "practical" Wing Chun or "applied" Wing Chun – or whatever you want to call it – without the extrapolation of the principles, concepts and tools of the forms is something other than Wing Chun.

The second and third elements of Wing Chun training are footwork and striking weapons. Of course, these originate in the forms – that's where the material for the proper way of moving and striking come from. Next up are the training drills. *Any practice at all is basically a training drill.* These drills are, once more, rational training applications of the concepts and principles put forth in the forms. Fifth, we study application tactics – such as how to deal with multiple opponents, how to defuse a situation and so forth.

But, again, it's the forms that give us the foundation upon which to build. It's been said that all of Western philosophy for the last 2,500 years has been a footnote on Plato. Well, whatever you think of that, all of Wing Chun is an extrapolation of the SLT form – especially its first four sections. Seriously. Get this down...and really understand it and you're on your way to being able to keep yourself as safe as possible through this incredibly effective fighting science.

So, in a nutshell, Wing Chun training can be seen in the

following:

- *Forms*
- *Footwork*
- *Striking tools*
- *Training drills*
- *Self-defense tactics*

In all, I assure you, this method of unarmed combat works. It will work for you so long as you understand the foundation and pour in the time to develop the proper tactical and muscle-memory. Much like using a gun, Wing Chun is based upon a brutally simple plan of firing and moving. If you're familiar with using a handgun, then you're already familiar with the need to be able to get shots down-range while *simultaneously* moving or using cover. Both the striking and the movement are your defense. To stand still is virtually unthinkable in real violence, so Wing Chun training will make you highly efficient at moving in confined spaces that are generally considered less than optimal for footwork – places like cluttered offices, parking garages, and hiking trails, just to name a few. Also, it will integrate that footwork into your ability to strike. It's a package-deal. Once you have this down, you'll be able to answer every attack with a superior counter-attack. That's the key.

With all of this said, you'll notice that Wing Chun, claiming to be a science of self-defense, is logically consistent both internally and externally. Once again, it isn't a good method for you to use if your interests are competitive fighting. If you want to box or do MMA, go do those disciplines. They are, when taught by qualified coaches, fine disciplines indeed. Wing Chun won't prepare you for them anymore than playing basketball will make you better at baseball. Sure, there's benefit to being in better shape from all that running and jumping, but it won't help you hit a curveball any better.

5

SELF-INFLICTED DAMAGE

The Safety of Wing Chun Training vs. the Destructiveness in Boxing, MMA, & Muay Thai

An often omitted, yet highly important consideration as to why Wing Chun should be your first and primary consideration for a self-defense system, pertains to the relative safety of the training.

Once more, let's look at firearms training for our example.

Any facility that offers firearm training grapples with the issue of safety. An accident with a gun, after all, is often deadly. If not deadly, then it's at least life-altering. For this reason, great attention is paid to making sure people don't do anything stupid. The four rules of gun safety, already referred to, are paramount – indeed, they're a gun-owner's gospel. Any deviation from one of these rules at a gun club will get the offender banned in short order – and for good reason too.

The point of it is, of course, that shooting someone or yourself by accident is quite antithetical to the whole enterprise. Imagine the insanity of acquiring a firearm for the purpose of not getting shot by a bad-guy and, behold, you shoot yourself instead. What an ironic tragedy.

We can and should apply this line of thinking to our hand-to-hand training.

This is where the comparison gets a bit interesting, though. A gun-club rarely has violations of its safety rules because they steadfastly profess them, monitor the members for their adherence to them and, in the main, take them – as they should – as matters of life and death. But far too many of us miss the dangers of doing the above listed sport-combat systems for self-defense. For the most part, the gun-club is a safer place for the average person looking for self-defense training than the MMA school. Why? Simply because the average training in the MMA school is personally damaging.

There are, naturally, variations across the spectrum. Some schools of boxing or Muay Thai will focus more upon the development of skill and health for its members than competition. That's great. But to those schools that really push contact sparring and "going hard" one must admit that such approaches are self-abusive in the name of self-defense.

Let's take a few examples.

The famous Muay Thai round kick is a fearsome weapon. It truly is. But it's also extremely damaging to the person wielding the weapon too. Simply put, hitting with all your power and using the top of your foot/shin bone to exact that power on a target is a curious bit of business. One should naturally pause and consider their course when upon joining a class for self-defense they're told that they must deaden the nerves in their leg in order to use it as a weapon. And how do you achieve this deadening goal? Well, by repeatedly pounding what was a weak part of your body into semi-hard objects until there is no more pain.

Or, let us take boxing into our consideration. There is no better system for teaching a person how to see and deal with punches coming at their face than boxing. But there is a productive way to do this – it's called coach-sparring. That is, a qualified coach spars with a newbie and taps, smacks and counters the student in an educational manner. Should the student get too over-daring or over-aggressive, the coach can and will put over a good blow here and there but even this is in the spirit of coaching. A student who continues to need "hard correction" will be counseled about the danger of their ways. They are there to learn to box, not brawl. If they can't break their habit, they're banished for their own safety.

But too many schools of boxing, unfortunately, have young, ignorant men leading other young men and they encourage hard-sparring between gym members. One shouldn't need a medical degree to deduce that repeated blows to the melon aren't good for brain health. The danger in boxing is that this damage is invisible, like a ravaging disease that lays dormant for years before manifesting itself. I will note that an individual interested in a boxing career – either amateur or pro – will certainly need to partake in "smokers" and hard sparring. But even these need to be regulated. Gym wars are the scourge of good boxing anyway. They turn students into brawlers rather than fistic scientists. But they also are the true reason a good many boxers end up brain damaged years after their tenure is up.

MMA gyms like to brag that they don't have to deal with brain injuries as boxing does. This may or may not be accurate but one does suppose that since their adherents take less blows to the head, this is probably true. Even still, it's a little like two men leaving a bar at night to drive home and the one bragging that he hasn't had nearly as much to drink as the other. The point is, both are drunk and gratuitous blows to the head to develop toughness in sparring is a perilous to one's future.

But MMA does have a host of other issues to consider as well.

In one nearby gym, an MMA fighter lost his two front teeth while sparring. He took a knee to the face. In sparring. For crying out loud! When I heard the story, it was told by a young man who was bragging about how tough the gym was. When I alerted the teller to the desultory facts that this was, first, something that was going to cost over $10,000 worth of dental work and, second, the fighter couldn't train now for probably a year or more, he was unfazed.

Other students of MMA, in the name of learning the game, have incurred all sorts of broken bones, blow-outs of the ACL, cuts, and various injuries. One fighter, a young man who had an off-and-on again amateur MMA career, when taken in the whole, received for his efforts the damage one would expect in a car-crash victim. What can be said of this in light of the fact that this poor fighter and so many others like him, paid for this abuse! I've seen memberships run upwards of $200 a month. By that reckoning, these poor, delusional souls, in a year's time, pay out a few thousand dollars, not to mention gas and incidentals, in order to assure that they're nearly crippled by the time they turn 50. What criminal could steal over $2000 from you? It's hardly likely unless you're a drug dealer, right? Such is the insanity of confusing modern sport-combat training with self-defense.

In fairness, I have encountered a few Wing Chun schools where they brag about having hurt each other in training. The principle should be, if the instructors don't talk to you both about the realism and the safety of the training, you should be concerned. And if, with no prompting from you, they talk about how tough the training is by reference to how many emergency-room visits they have after class, you're advised to seek an exit.

Once again, to be clear, if your goal is self-defense, engaging in training that's self-destructive is nonsensical at best and sociopathic at worst. Proper Wing Chun can and will make use of modern sport training. But at every turn the coaches should logically seek the wise mix of realism and safety through proper forms, footwork, technique, training drills and tactics. Modern special warfare units and military training is a good guide in that they use a multitude of stressful training drills that are safe. To prepare for war by having war would leave any military unit unfit in short order. To prepare for self-defense by fighting is similarly illogical.

==To be realistic is not to be confused with being real.== In any event, trying to be real is impossible because anything we do in a school is going to be specific to that environment. Hard sparring in a gym is a way to *pressure test* - sure. But in order to do that safely we must alter the equation with gloves and protective gear. One simply cannot fully pressure test groin kicks and bare-knuckle punches. Therefore, I recommend light sparring with gloves under professional supervision in order to develop timing and accuracy. Going beyond that is detrimental to the health of the participants and gives them a false sense of all-out fighting.

Anyway, as you can see, though the aforementioned, and quite popular combat sports, are excellent in their domain, they often cause injury to the student. Also, the physical demands of these systems – the upkeep – is considerable. A young man of 25 and a mature man of 50 are different in their physical abilities to recover from high-stress workouts. Wing Chun, properly understood and trained, is something that should help develop fitness while not going too far. Balance is essential.

With this in consideration, even if one can derive greater self-defense skills from the combative sports like MMA, boxing and Thai kickboxing, and that is debatable, the toll of the training must be seen for what it is. Proper Wing Chun training can provide a person with fine self-defense skills in a relatively safe manner and the training can be maintained for years. The damage of the other systems, on the other hand, often prohibit the trainee from pursuing such training in all but the most athletic years of their lives.

This brings up the obvious questions as to how effective the training is if it cannot be maintained past the peak years of one's prime. After all, a man of 45 would still need use of a self-defense system even if his body can no longer absorb the heavy pounding required by sport-based systems. What then can he do? A good test of a self-defense method ought to be whether or not you can do it at 60 years-old. If the training requires a perpetual youth then it's certainly unrealistic. For some reason, this is often omitted as people consider a self-defense system.

Personally, I know several former MMA fighters who, now in their 40's, are struggling with the injuries of their heyday.

Thus, for a self-defense method to be considered scientific, it must encompass these auxiliary issues as well as their actual fighting effectiveness. It's not my contention that the other methods mentioned are incapable of defending you. I do profess, however, that Wing Chun does so just as well and, in many cases, better than those methods, and is also safer and practicable over the long haul. By neglecting these aspects, sport-based trainees are like a man who buys a bazooka for home-defense. Sure, the bazooka is a fine weapon but it's not so well suited for the task at hand. It will absolutely kill the bad guy. But that's not all there is to it, right?

6

THE LOGIC & HISTORY OF WING CHUN TACTICS

A DEFENSE AGAINST SPORT CRITICS

A very frequent - and sometimes fervent - charge against Wing Chun is that it's not tested in sparring. Detractors say that it looks and sounds logical but all you're doing is practice and unless you can perform these moves in hard sparring, it won't work. We could easily refute this line of reasoning by noting the futility of testing eye-gouges and throat strikes on actual training partners instead of training equipment. We could also point out the disparity between mutual combat (stalking) and a sudden, violent encounter and leave it at that. But, in respect to the questioner, ascribing to him the honor of best-of-intentions, let me add the following.

Our approach is to use training drills to develop proper tactical skill, accuracy and timing in as safe a manner as possible. Each drill is calibrated so as to develop and enhance a fighting quality. Working the bare-knuckle punching, low-line kicks with shoes on, throat-strike, eye-gouge, and head-butt is done on training equipment. This must be done so that the trainee develops the necessary reflexive skill to actually use those techniques in combat. Sparring drills, likewise, are invaluable to develop timing and accuracy. We prefer boxing for this as it delivers the goods we want (timing and accuracy against a moving opponent) while also being limited enough to be safe and, importantly, not greatly alter our fighting structure.

The goal with such sparring is, therefore, control. Much like a sniper working on position. He doesn't shoot people for practice. He has to separate the two. He trains to conceal himself and - separately - he trains to shoot accurately. The point is that, once he has position, his shot can take out the target. We see boxing in a similar way. The Wing Chun fighter spars lightly in order to get experience seeing strikes and to work on getting position. Once he has position, he knows that throat-strikes, head-butts, groin strikes, shin kicks and eye-gouges will work.

The key, like with the sniper, is getting it set up. Over-emphasis on sparring is actually counter-productive as the student will be inclined to discover elaborate strategies to defeat his/her partner. These will be stalking strategies as opposed to counter-attack tactics that are needed in self-defense. *Add to this that the safety equipment and limited targeting will change the cost-benefit equation and you begin to understand why sparring for any reason other than the acquisition of timing and accuracy is detrimental to logical self-defense.*

Now, this should convince the skeptic. The logic is clear and non-contradictory. If I'm wrong, then sparring is fighting and that's preposterous. Consequently, the hard-sparring case against Wing Chun collapses. But there's more. It's not as though we don't have past experience to draw from as well.

It's well documented from the writings of self-defense and dueling experts of the past few centuries that there was a particular group of fighters to be avoided. These less than esteemed, but highly feared men were called *rough-and-tumble* fighters. Indeed, the highly skilled and cultivated fighters of the day, including the great Colonel Thomas Hoyer Monstery, that renowned duelist and warrior of the 19th Century, were less than enamored with these fighters. Many considered them barely above the rank of savages. But feared they were. Monstery himself advised against ever fighting these men. He said,

"*Generally, my advice is keep clear of rough-and-tumble fighters, or shoot them down, for they are horrible beings, bent on murdering or maiming their fellow creatures, and worthy of no better treatment than men give to wolves - that is bullet or steel.*"

Why were these fighters so feared - and loathed? It was reported that fighters of that style were literally *no-holds-barred* and men were "sure to lose a finger, an eye, or a nose, and to be bitten or gouged in a horrible manner..." (*from Monstery's Self-Defense for Ladies and Gentleman*).

This should draw our attention because the masters of the past, unlike today, weren't dealing with sport rules for the most part. They were men that fought with bare fists, with knives, swords, and sticks. They were the type of men that make contemporary manly men look like sissies. Many of today's so-called fighters are, for better or worse, sport fighters and they are conditioned to fight according to rules. These duelists, quite naturally, sometimes died from their competitions so it's fair to say, in the very least, that they had a view of combative things that should speak truth to us across the decades and centuries as we face an ever more violent society.

But it wasn't just close-range foul tactics like biting, butting and gouging that made such fighters formidable. They also kicked. Low. At the shins and knees. Most of us in America are ignorant of our history, so this needs to be pointed out. "Purring", which is what the art of low-line kicking was called in the British Isles, was naturally brought to America. *The New York Times*, reporting on a match between Robert Tavish and David McWilliams in Camden, New Jersey in 1883, referred to purring a scientific shin-kicking. The loser often suffered a broken leg or was kicked into submission - his legs ground up "like hamburger meat." Much of this damage was done in close too - from a clinch!

So, against the charge from sporting fighters that Wing Chun isn't tested - I offer not just the logic of the system but this bit of history too. These rough fellows were, for all intents and purposes, fighting in the manner and style we're discussing. This means that the charge that these tactics are untested is illogical and unhistorical. These fighters of the past were eye-gougers and head-butters; they were dirty close-range warriors that attacked the jaw, the eyes, the neck and throat. They held and hit. And they hit low. They had no regard for decency. They would even bite whenever and wherever they could. Monstery and others cautioned that if you had long hair, they would grab hold of you and bite your face! Yes...this was a class of fighters in that day. Ruthless and savage but highly efficient in their tactics. To win a fight against these men often relegated the victor to some sort of serious injury. They were best to be left alone. Think of the famous fight between Bill "The Butcher" Poole and John Morrissey in New York in 1854. No one wanted to fight such men.

Well, my friends, as we seek to engage contemporary threats it's best that we live in the real world. We should note that these past duelists were often concerned with honor in combat. Those men were living in a time when people had a code and that code affected even the way men behaved in combat. Incidentally, it was noted in newspaper accounts of the day that some Chinese immigrants, when fighting, fought a very "dirty" game too – much like the rough-and-tumble group. We can have a debate on the reasons for the West's collapse of virtue and morality some other time, but it's unthinkable for the modern warrior to insist it isn't happening. When I was growing up in a poor town in Upstate New York where there were plenty of fights among the young men, myself included, it was unthinkable to hit a downed opponent or someone who said, "Uncle." The witnesses were sure to intercede – they would police themselves, if you will – if one party continued to put it on a boy unable and/or unwilling to defend himself.

Those days are, sadly, regrettably, as gone as most of the vestiges of old America. Like I said, you can say what you want about the changes of this country in the last 20-30 years. You can say that we are stamping out injustices by eradicating the old moral codes. You are welcome to that opinion but there can be no denying that this is a more dangerous place than it was when I was a child. This isn't the same land where an 8-year-old boy could go off from home for the entire day, come home when the street lights came on, and the parents not worry. That would get most parents arrested today. It's unthinkable. Because everyone is doing what's right in their own eyes, pornography, violence, and lack of respect for authority rule the day. People seem to have confused liberty with anarchy and, thus, they've replaced rule of law with lawlessness. All of this, quite naturally, means that if you're in a fight, you are much less likely to be in a fair fight than in the recent past. It's more like those days a century or two ago, when life was dirty, brutal and - tragically - often very short.

It's in this world that we live and it's in this world that a person must consider his or her self-defense method.

And it's here that I wish to tell you that Wing Chun should be your choice. It should be your choice exactly because it's a *science of infighting*, which is to say that it's a logical and comprehensive system very much like what the rough-and-tumblers were doing a century ago. This alone should make any warrior stand up and consider Wing Chun over other systems.

A number of years ago a martial arts teacher from a nearby school paid me a visit. He identified himself as a grandmaster. This was because, as he explained, he had modified the original Karate system he'd learned so much that it was an entirely new system, thus granting him the coveted title *grandmaster*. For the next several days afterwards, incidentally, I identified myself, and expected to be addressed by one and all, as *"Your Worshipfulness-ship."* That was, of course, something like what Hans Solo called Princess Leia in his first go-round with her on the big, bad *Death Star*. We all had lots of fun.

Sorry. I digress.

Anyway, aside from delusions of grandeur, my erstwhile visitor told me all about his vaunted system and how thorough it was in dispatching one and all. It was a complete system, he said. How complete? Well, he counted over a thousand techniques. But then, without any prompting at all from me, he declared, "But don't get me wrong...in a real fight I wouldn't mess around – I'd poke him in the eye and break his knee."

Fascinating.

Now, naturally, one wonders what all the other techniques are that he won't use or, in his own words, mess around with. One wonders how much free time a man has when he can devote his life to the mastery of a thousand techniques that are "messing around". Perhaps he could have devoted such time and energies to other endeavors more productive – like carpentry or landscaping or winning and holding Euro-Asia in *Risk*. Or, if he really wanted to waste time, he could have become a writer. But I digress again. Quite sorry.

This seems to be the majority report, however. Every conversation I have with martial artist, boxer, MMA dude, and civilian alike, there is the same refrain: *"If I'm in a real fight...I'll go after the eyes and all that stuff..."* This seems, in my humble estimation, as ubiquitous as the proverbial, "the check's in the mail" or, when I'd ask a girl for her phone number, "...just give me yours...I'll call you." (That only happened once or twice. Seriously.)

The truth of the matter is, though, that men and women hardly ever rise to the level of their challenge – especially in a violent encounter. You're only as good as your practice. And if you never practice something, there's little to no chance that you'll pull it off effectively in a fight. And this is exactly where Wing Chun should interest anyone desirous of protecting themselves. I mean, if you want to break boards, go break boards. That's fun. I get it. Plus, the school makes money from you having to buy all those innocent, never bothered anyone pieces of wood. And if you want to roll around on a mat (and streets and parking lots are full of nice padded mats, right?) then go do that too. It's fun. I understand. But if you're thinking of maximum self-protection then don't kid yourself. What you master in practice is what you'll do in a fight. Wing Chun is a science of the very stuff everyone else says they're going to do. It's that simple.

Some Basic Facts

. . .

When I'm asked about Wing Chun the first thing I tell people is that it's a true self-defense method. Generally, I'm asked this in environments like the office at my school or at a convenience store where someone asks me about the shirt I'm wearing. You'll note that you're hardly ever in a nice, safe, padded environment; you're generally surrounded by stuff – and hard stuff at that, like counters, tables, windows, cars and pavement. Besides, if you're in a padded environment all the time, you're either insane or a sport fighter. But I repeat myself again.

So, we have limited room to move. That's very important to understand. And the room you have to move in is wrought with potential dangers. For example, falling on a mat or getting slammed against a cage doesn't quite compare to falling down a flight of stairs or striking your precious noggin on the edge of a table. Wing Chun, therefore, is a science of close-range footwork, pivoting and shifting. It's a transportation system designed for the urban jungle, not the ring or cage. Imagine vintage Tyson moving, coming in fast and using angles – very aggressive but smart too. Wing Chun footwork is designed to take the fight to the enemy while not letting him face you directly. It's a system of angle stepping, shifting and pivoting that seeks to nullify the other guy's offense while setting up your own.

Next, it's a system of attacking *and defending* the body's center-mass and most vulnerable targets.

For example, I often explain Wing Chun to new students with a little demonstration. I tell them that I'm going to grab their eyes and that they should try and stop me. Well, this isn't the garden-variety way most people think to start a fight. People are generally quite taken aback by this as it seems particularly barbaric. But to the Wing Chun fighter, dying or being maimed by a criminal is what's barbaric. Therefore, any means at our disposal to avoid such is a rather good idea. Anyway, as I shoot forward, untrained people are rarely quick enough to block or get out of the way of the rapid and economical attack and, in short order, I have thumbs on both eyes (not hurting them, of course…we don't do that until after they sign up). If they do manage to avoid the initial burst, they do so with poor mechanical structure. They lean back or pull to the side awkwardly, leaving them off balance – easily pushed or pulled in that unsafe environment of hard objects. Or they get an arm in the way. But this is momentary because Wing Chun's unique in-fighting training drills teaches one to instinctively clear obstructions and move on to the target with minimal fuss. Perhaps at this point I don't get the eyes, though. Maybe it's the throat, or neck, or driving the jaw back. Whatever. Wing Chun teaches you to let them help you hit them. Indeed, by not fighting force with force, you go where the openings are.

Anyway, in short order you have an example of why Wing Chun is so effective. Unlike the rough-and-tumble guys of the past, where they often traded blows, and everyone was injured (kind of like a modern Presidential election) Wing Chun teaches you to control the enemy while hurting him, thus obliterating his ability to respond in kind. It's simple, but not easy. There's a clear system that's more comprehensive than just gouging an eye. After all, if you think you're just going to poke a guy in the eye, what happens if that's his plan too? We remember that this seems to be everyone's stated goal. That being the case, our system of self-defense should assist us in not only attacking the enemy's weakest targets but also in simultaneously defending our own. This is no small point, incidentally. If we both walk away maimed and/or blind, I can hardly count that as a victory. An eye for an eye is hardly a good fighting tactic.

Wing Chun, therefore, is a brilliant close-range system that teaches the simultaneous nullification of your enemy's attack and the delivery of your own. It does this with an ingenious methodology that is logically structured and tactically brilliant. With all due respect to the great Wong Shun Leung, who once remarked that the best form of self-defense would be to become invisible, but if you can't do that, learn Wing Chun – I've always preferred a more effective way of dealing with enemies if possible. Remember the first Terminator movie? Now that's how you deal with an enemy! Send a life-like homicidal robot back in time to kill his mother. That's the ticket! Of course, that's rather hard to do considering that you need both a time machine and a homicidal robot. More still, that whole shebang would likely be rather cost prohibitive too and only rich people would have them (look out Bernie Sanders!!). Sadly, that being the case, I think Wing Chun is your go-to self-defense method. Both logic and history concur.

7

PHILOSOPHERS OF THE FIST
THEORY & PRACTICE

"*The nation that will insist on drawing a broad line of demarcation between the fighting man and the thinking man is liable to find its fighting done by fools and its thinking done by cowards.*" William Francis Butler

A martial artist is a philosopher. He isn't a soldier by definition, nor is he a fighter, though he may be employed in either vocation. A martial artist is a philosopher of the fist who isn't told when to fight by a commanding officer, nor how and where. He isn't a sport-fighter either. And he certainly isn't a barbarian and bully. No, a martial artist is rightly a philosopher of the fist.

We must understand the critical difference because if a martial artist isn't a specific thing and is one of those previous things then martial arts is not really something at all. This is my objection to something like *Krav Maga*. What is that except a hodge-podge of techniques for self-protection in a vacuum? It's the perfect Western martial art – a system devoid of sticky questions like ethics and metaphysics. *"Just do this...then that...don't worry about the broader subject of violence or of ethics...or of what it is to be a warrior...just do it."* It's the quest for performance without foundation, for truth without principle, for excellence without true commitment.

Instead, a philosopher is a lover of wisdom. To be wise is to understand the broader themes of life (like origins, meaning, ethics, and destiny). A philosopher of the fist, therefore, is someone who understands that violence is the central thing wrong with human interaction. The initiation of violence against the innocent isn't some bacteria, or a hurricane, or other natural force that terrorizes mankind. Rather, it's a result of incongruent (and ultimately evil) human volition. The free-will of man that results in such initiation of violence is guided by false premises. All aggressive people in history – from Hitler, Stalin, Castro and Mao, all the way to the bully in middle-school – attempt to morally and intellectually justify their ethically aberrant behavior. For this reason, the martial artist accepts the responsibility to grow in truth[1].

Violence, in and of itself can't be immoral or else, once again, our entire enterprise collapses. Since it's a consequence of contradictory moral reasoning, the initiation of force, acts as the one and supreme act of immorality upon earth. A hurricane isn't immoral. Morality is a function of moral beings who have been endowed with choice and consciousness. Thus, the denial of one's proper nature – their choice, either directly through violence or indirectly through fraud or threat, is life's primary social issue. If all people were to truly "treat others as they want to be treated" there would certainly be no violence. But since there is, the only rational/moral response is self-defense.

In this way, self-defense training is an extremely moral and loving discipline so long as it's kept in this strict context. To train in violence properly[2], therefore, one must have the right moral and philosophical foundation. To omit this standard from the training is an exceedingly dangerous thing to do.

Furthermore, the martial artist must take responsibility for their personal life, attempting to live for the profound virtues of God in this world – pursuing excellence, beauty and peace. To merely be an expert in violence is a shallow thing indeed if that skill isn't directed to higher causes in the service of truth. If people were automatons and not possessors of reason and free-will, then the entire subject would be superfluous. If violence was just another fact of nature and man wasn't a moral image-bearer of their creator God, then all this training to stop it would be arbitrary. But man is different from everything else in nature – especially and including animals. A bear that attacks a person hasn't done anything immoral and we know it, despite how unfair the fight is. The bear doesn't care, nor is he supposed to care, about the weight class difference between itself and the person. But we know, at a level so elementary that it ought to tell us that God has written His truth on our hearts, that a trained fighter attacking an old lady (or a child) is horrifically immoral.

You see, the entire issue of self-defense only makes sense if this is a moral universe[3]. The abnegation of sound moral philosophy by the martial artist is, therefore, profoundly regrettable. It's on these grounds that we should reject self-defense as a mere *operational science* devoid of the deeper moral and philosophical considerations.

All of this said, most of us today think that being ideological is a thing to be avoided; we're raised to believe that having set principles makes us inflexible. But this itself is a set principle, isn't it? The dirty little secret is that there's no avoiding the solemn responsibility to hold true and moral foundational principles. The people who tell you that you shouldn't have them are really only trying to get you to accept theirs - and uncritically at that. I'll do no such thing. I'm going to unabashedly sell you the Wing Chun foundation and principles exactly because they're logical. If they aren't then it's incumbent upon us to reject them.

Furthermore, not having a clear and logical set of principles from which you act guarantees that you'll be, not free, but willfully ignorant. But ignorant people routinely make major errors in their judgments about life. This type of thing is hardly consistent with the path of a martial artist who seeks, in the principle of life, to guard himself against the force and/or trickery of enemies, and the self-destruction that comes from lack of personal control and respect.

Our age is one of anti-philosophy and, consequently, anti-morality. But all of life is ethical insofar as every decision we make has an ethical component to it. This is especially the case when our actions are directly dealing with others. In this light, the martial artist must be a student of proper moral philosophy. Any moral philosophy that provides for the initiation of force against another is manifestly evil. All martial artists absolutely must swear off such violation of the freedom of their neighbors as a matter of first principle. Any person who believes that the violation of consent is a small matter that's contextual and, therefore, may be ignored as circumstances allow, is a moral monster. Any person who doesn't have the courage of this conviction (won't use force personally) but votes for their proxy to violate their neighbor's free-will is both a moral monster and a coward.

We repeat: the premise of martial art training is self-defense and this rests upon the moral foundation of civil/political freedom. For this reason, all martial artists must reject any personal and/or political convictions that result in the violation of their neighbor's consent. All human conflict – whether in business, politics, families, schools, etc.[4] – stems from this core issue. If everyone actually treats their neighbor as they want to be treated, there would be no need for self-defense.

If every martial artist is taught this essential and logically consistent moral philosophy and holds to it so much as they are able by God's grace, the impact on society would be enormous. The schools have largely abandoned sound reasoning and proper, God-given morality. In this vacuum, we have a storm of violence and anarchy brewing. The dark clouds of this reckoning are gathering ominously on our not too distant horizon. Considering how many martial art schools there are, one can imagine what would happen if all accepted their true calling and taught this philosophy of the fist along with the physical art.

Years ago, I was required by my home state of South Carolina to take a concealed carry course in order to legally carry my firearm. Millions of people do this in America every year. The instructor I had was a retired law-enforcement official from Spartanburg County. He was a very engaging man. He was an expert in his field – knowledgeable, full of experience, and very personable too. During the course, he covered the legal requirements pertaining to the use of a firearm. This was needed and extremely valuable information.

What was missing, however, were the bedrock principles of self-defense. Our culture simply doesn't want to talk about them anymore. Some omit talk of God and morality because they're afraid of offending others. One wonders, however, how God feels about being thought of so little that men of arms prefer to dismiss Him rather than make a fellow image-bearer unhappy. You can hardly imagine a scene where a Marine captain gives his troops orders but declines to tell them where the orders came from because some of them don't like the General from which they originated. That unit would soon break down and so is ours – our culture – due to our intransigence and hatred of God's moral order. Those who claim that they can still act morally without God are actually not saying what they think they are. They're stating that the universe is ultimately moral and that *they know it*. But how could this be possible if the world is a mere accident, governed by chance?

So, I did the course and I've been trained in the legality of carrying a deadly weapon yet, sadly, nothing has been said of morality. And nothing was said because the culture doesn't want to hear about moral authority that's above their own. Thus, we're all little gods since we all are determined to decide right and wrong on our terms. And some of us are armed. Do you see where this is headed? A world of little gods will war with one another. They must.

This is why this chapter must logically be included in a self-defense book. And this is why we must be *priests* and *philosophers of the fist* - swearing off any aggression toward our neighbor and accepting the responsibilities of living with honor.

8

WING CHUN: THE PHILOSOPHICAL FIGHTING SCIENCE

Some of my cohorts in Wing Chun refer to their way as the *science of in-fighting*. This use of the word science – and its general overuse in today's world – needs some clarification. The reason for this is pretty simple. We've all heard a friend say something like, *"If we can send men to the moon, why can't we...?"* This comes up when the friend is exasperated by some limitation they've encountered in their life. It's an obvious question in one regard because we're surrounded by great technological achievements. Heck, I'm writing on one right now (a MacBook Pro) and it's awesome.

The problem is, who is this *we* we're talking about? A lot of people I know couldn't survive for a week in the woods. You see, the presence of advanced sciences in one field doesn't necessarily mean advances in other areas too. And one of them is in fighting sciences. Sure, we have all these cool toys and gadgets but we're basically the same biped that strolled the streets of Athens and Rome centuries ago. Yeah, sure, I can drive my Toyota Tundra at high speeds while listening to satellite radio and sipping some awesome coffee, but that doesn't make me – the human being – more advanced than, say, Spartacus. You might even say that Spartacus, despite his lack of a Tundra and a classic rock station, was a more formidable warrior than just about anyone I could encounter today.

So, the point is, I get worried about the use of the word science because it covers quite a bit of ground. What type of science are we talking about? Molecular science? Medical science? Computer science? Plus, moderns use it all the time to hide their arrogance and sense of superiority. It's like the friend that complains about people going to the moon, yet we can't cure the common cold. It doesn't matter to him that he might be as dumb as a bag of rocks – in his mind "science" should solve all problems. This is the key to it. The use of science today generally has a sort of idolatrous ring to it. It means that "they" (scientists I guess) should have an answer for a problem I can't solve.

I prefer, therefore, to say that Wing Chun is a system of logical principles. These principles have to be applied in real life. This shifts the burden to where it should be: onto us. The problem is that a good many people today have been educated into philosophical imbecility; they've gained skill in certain disciplines, but this makes them educated dunces if they're not also trained in logic and philosophy. And what is logic except for the art of non-contradictory identification? Logic is the correct apprehension of the facts of reality. Without logic, science is impossible. Isn't it ironic that as technological advances have increased, the population has grown more irrational? Ah, but that's another book altogether.

All of this said, to be a true warrior you must be a true philosopher – a philosopher of the fist; you must be inherently logical, ruthlessly rooting out error and contradiction. After all, to arrive at a contradiction in one's evaluation of reality – in any endeavor – is to run headlong into *unreality*. To be wrong about something is to be illogical or, if you will, to be *unreal*. Well, lack of realism may very well get you killed, which is why every warrior cares more about truth (arrived at logically, through non-contradictory identification) than for *tradition*. This should be the way we see Wing Chun. We should see it as that which is combatively logical. If we do something irrational in regard to the goal of keeping ourselves as safe as possible, we aren't doing Wing Chun because Wing Chun is a set of logical self-protection principles that need to be applied in a sudden violent encounter.

If my computer isn't working, I have a specific thing that has a specific problem which is restricting a specific function. A computer does what it does. But a logical fighting method isn't a computer. A good deal of issues might arise which can alter the equations. For example, a fight may take place on a beach, in a stairwell, an elevator, in a car, etc. And for each of these scenarios there are a multitude of variables that might influence the application of the logical principles. Let's say I have a hot coffee in my hand and I'm attacked. Well, the logic of throwing coffee in the dude's face and then kicking him in the jollies isn't bad. But maybe instead of coffee I'm carrying my new computer - or my baby! That plan doesn't work if I've got something I wouldn't want to throw. So, you see, it's okay to view Wing Chun as a science but that might – just might – convey to you that it's a set thing, not living and requiring interpretation and re-interpretation. I'm just trying to be clear because the majority seem to have a much higher view of science than philosophy and they've arrived at that conclusion precisely because they've been instructed in the ways of bad philosophy.

But philosophy precedes science for the very reason that the questions of *why* and *what for* are paramount in every endeavor.

This is to say that the practice of anything is the practice of some theory or another. Every single thing you do derives from a core principle. Everything. No kidding. The problem is that most people never define their principles.

If you're raised in modern-day Saudi Arabia or Iran, one logically presumes that you've been brought up – intellectually, that is – in soil that's fundamentally Islamic. If you were raised, on the other hand, in 18th century New England at the height of the Great Awakening, the intellectual soil your mind grew in was very Christian – and a very

Calvinistic, Protestant Christianity at that. Well, likewise, if you are raised in the modern West you are most certainly a relativist.

I bring this up because it directly impacts our worldview. To be sure, all of us are philosophers. Rail against that all you want and be as frivolous with your mind as you wish, but there's no escaping the fact that to live even one day on this planet requires a belief structure regarding what is *ultimately true*. Indeed, you have no choice in the matter; the question is whether or not you'll be a good philosopher or a poor one. Most people, obviously, by virtue of their neglect, choose to be poor philosophers. The real tragedy of this, incidentally, is that it relegates them to living an unfocused life, guided by principles chosen randomly that are often mutually exclusive.

It's terribly easy to simply accept the dominant worldview (philosophy) passed down through our dominant institutions. In America the strongest institution isn't the family anymore – it's basically the media and the school systems. And the clear philosophy of the American media and school system is that of self-worship and moral relativism. It's smuggled into every little thing we do and learn. Many apostles of relativistic philosophy prefer to call their belief *pluralism*, which is to say basically the same thing without going as far. Pluralists are really cowardly relativists. The issue is: relativism is the belief that there is no such thing as an absolute truth and that, moreover, truth is a social construct, not a metaphysical (ultimate) fact.

Ah, but you say this discussion has nothing to do with martial art. I understand your angst so please stay with me. A philosopher is – or at least should be – a lover of truth and everything about self-defense better be reality and truth. That's the critical issue. If you've been brought up as a relativist – or you haven't really even thought about it – you are likely approaching life with a very subjective mindset. This means that you think truth is whatever you say it is. But, listen, that's all dangerously silly. Relativism is a fundamentally flawed philosophy that is *necessarily false*. That is to say it *absolutely must be false*. For example:

. . .

If you profess that there is no absolute truth, you've just professed one.

If you say that no person can really know the truth for certain, you've just claimed that you know that truth.

If you contend that absolute claims are exclusionary, you've just made an exclusionary claim yourself.

You see, relativism and all its ugly, evil step-children, pluralism included, is like being in a fight, getting taken down, and then pulling the pin on a grenade in order to beat the guy. Relativism blows up knowledge; it makes all knowledge and reasoning impossible. This is important because we're dealing with the ultimate of reality when we're dealing with violence. I've always thought that the martial artist and warrior was the true philosopher for the very reason that, unlike academics, politicians, and abstract artists, we must directly face the consequences of our ideas. If our ideas suck, well it's our beat-down. Philosophy is not, despite what we've made of it, some ivory tower pursuit of tenured professors who rarely teach classes (that's for grad students anyway!) or have contact with the real world. Certainly not! As warriors, we're interested in philosophy because we're interested in truth and we're interested in truth because we intend to deal with reality – specifically, the reality of violence. And violence tolerates no pretenders. It's the ultimate acid test of ideas.

Many people, confused by this contemporary sham, give up altogether on ideas and philosophy. They think it's all nonsense and so they live as "practical" men. But, in reality, there's no more practical a man than the man of truth. Furthermore, what is a practical man or woman? They are someone who believes they are dealing with reality – with truth. That's always the issue, isn't it? Napoleon, who knew a little something about warfare, once said that *"in war, the moral is to the physical as three to one."* We must never forget that we are body/soul, or mind/body; a warrior with the wrong mindset because he has abdicated his responsibility to think in correspondence to reality, is half a fighter. You must embrace a life of the mind and, therefore, endeavor to think logically about life. Anything less is immoral and, straight to our point, dangerous.

So, these ideas that Wing Chun espouses are based on true, logical principles derived from sound philosophy and, yes, despite relativistic bantering to the contrary, we can know the truth.

Attack of the "Practical" Martial Arts

The other reason I bring this up is because many people are flocking to training systems that tout themselves as reality based. They brashly proclaim that they aren't traditional – they're modern and free of all the baggage of the old systems. But this is a lie because every practice is based on a core belief. Traditional systems, if they were ineffective, were thus not because they were traditional but because they were illogical. So how has the modern system, just by virtue of being newer, become more logical? Just because something is younger doesn't make it automatically more effective.

Wing Chun sees the problem this way: the other systems often fail because people have not been trained in true, logical principles – which are adaptable – to the point that they're reflexive. A system that has a move for everything, but no core principles is a convoluted, unusable mess. If I have a move for this attack, another for that, and another for that, things are going to get over-complicated in a hurry. It's like teaching division one problem at a time without giving the formula. Imagine: *"903 divided by 3 is 301. Repeat. Repeat..."*

You'd never learn division that way. There are too many variances. What if the question is "707 divided by 18?" You won't know the answer because you only learned one problem by memory but not the *formula*. Fighting is similar. You need to learn the root principles – the core theory as well as the practice. That's Wing Chun.

Interestingly, this is precisely why we don't see more Wing Chun in the marketplace of self-defense. Think about it: it's far easier to teach people to *do this, then that, and then...and then...*and give them a false sense of security. Proper Wing Chun, however, being a system of concepts, requires a little more thought from both the instructors and the students. So, therefore, I am certainly not writing this book to tell you that Wing Chun is easy in the sense that you can do it without being both a logical thinker and a hard worker. On the contrary, I'm writing it to tell you the opposite. It's the fighting method of the thinking person, the conceptual person, and the dedicated worker who trains to conform action to proper, logical theory. I'm saying that Wing Chun is the method of philosophy in action – thus creating men and women of the mind and the fist; philosopher-warriors, not one or the other.

The fact that these systems are so rabidly anti-theoretical is precisely because they've grown in the soil of relativistic, anti-theoretical culture. Some of us, in response to this error, swing wildly in the other direction and embrace the tin-god of traditionalism. We'll address that in our last chapter.

Since I teach martial arts for a living, I'm often asked to do self-defense courses and/or lectures for different groups. Quite frankly, I have a love/hate relationship with such offers. On the one hand, I love going out and meeting people and educating them to the virtues of true martial arts. On the other, however, it's quite often frustrating because many people are lazy and persist, despite my teaching to the contrary, that they can just learn a move or two and then move on with their life. They think, "Ah, well, I have a house, a car, a job...I probably need a self-defense move too...lemme look into that."

But under stress, especially violent stress, you aren't likely to rise to the level of your challenge – you're going to sink to the level of your discipline. We need to always remember that. Mastery is not doing something right once – *it's having to think about it to do it wrong*. For this reason, I bristle at the notion that you can give someone a move or two and they'll be okay in a violent encounter. The truth is the opposite. I spend my time alerting them to the necessities of awareness and avoidance. Then, I tell them, if you're so unlucky to be attacked despite efforts to avoid being an easy target, just fight! Don't worry about doing something specific. Just go with your natural self-preservation instincts, try and keep your chin down, and fight. Then, if you get a chance, run and escape.

Invariably, someone will ask for a definitive self-defense move, despite how clearly I tell them that specific responses not trained for will very likely fail in the chaotic stress of combat. "But what should I do if...?"

"Just fight."

"But what if...?"

"Listen," I counsel them, "unless you're going to actually train, it's a lie for me to tell you that you're going to hear something from me today and then maybe a year from now, you get attacked, and somehow execute a specific move against a specific opponent in a specific way. You won't. It won't happen. That will give you a false impression and confidence. The better way to go is to do everything I tell you about being aware and use evasive tactics as best you can. Then, if you're still attacked, fight like hell. Tell yourself that. That's the truth. If you aren't trained specifically and you try and be specific under pressure, the odds are high that you'll fail. You're better off just going with your natural response – crazy and wild though it might be – than trying to do a move I'll show you right now that you'll never practice."

But they saw some *Karate* expert do this or that, they protest.

"Maybe they can do that. I don't know. But I tell you, fighting is ugly business. A lot of these demos you see are dangerous because they're designed to be appealing in order to drum up confidence and, therefore, business for the style and school. If you really want to be a martial artist, that's great. I can help you. But if you have no intention of learning and devoting yourself to practice, admit that to yourself. Self-defense isn't like a jacket. You can't just walk into the store and buy one. It isn't a garment...it's something you become. You become the weapon. If you aren't willing to do that, admit it to yourself and work instead on awareness and avoidance."

That's pretty much verbatim what happens at a lot of these events. Of course, the questioner is often rather irritated with me as a result.

Carl Trueman, a great social critic and theologian/philosopher, has written that the West, and America especially, defines itself through consumerism and entertainment. We live, as Trueman calls it, in the pleasure dome. Our thoughts are often expended upon entertainment and consumption rather than production. I'm certainly not excluding myself from this, please know. My house is made of the same social glass as yours more than likely, so I don't mean to throw stones. What I mean to say is that we're all prone to eschew mental effort because it's easier in our amazingly affluent culture to watch a movie. It's easy to be entertained. In short, it's easier to let things be done for us. Michael Phelps, the renowned Olympian, is reputed to have said that most people focus on winners whereas he, a winner, focused on winning. I'd like to think that this is in support of our point. I'd like to think that he means by this that you aren't truly going to achieve excellence if you approach life as a spectator and consumer. Certainly, in Wing Chun this is absolutely the case.

Parenthetically, this is also the reason why the 2nd Amendment is under attack. When it was written, the assumption was that America would not have a standing army but, rather, a society of *citizen-soldiers* who took the responsibility to arm and train themselves for the common defense. We note that most state laws of the time required that citizens of the militia (read that: all able-bodied men basically) would provide their own arms. In short, it was assumed that a free person was a responsible person. It was assumed that certain things, if one was to be free, could not be outsourced. One was free only insofar as he could speak, write, worship, assemble peacefully and, critically, defend himself. This is why debating a gun-control advocate these days is a frustrating thing. If it isn't assumed that self-defense is your responsibility first and foremost, then the idea of carrying and *being* a weapon is bizarre to you.

But this is the core of martial arts. Miss this critical point and you miss what it is to be both a martial artist and a free person.

. . .

So, Wing Chun will not tell you what to do in a hundred different scenarios, one move at a time. It will teach you how to think, rather than what to do in a vacuum; it will break you free from anti-conceptualism so that you're free to adapt to those hundred scenarios. Wing Chun will make you into the weapon by teaching you true and logical core concepts and how to apply them in variable circumstances. This will account for exactly why Wing Chun is taught so differently than other systems. It's taught thus because it is a conceptual methodology. Critically, it's a system of principles and structure rather than pragmatism. Pragmatism can see that something worked, but not why - which leaves us at the mercy of experience rather than principle. But experience is a deficient teacher in that she gives the test first and the lesson afterward. We must never forget that.

In modern politics it's common to ask someone about an election and find out which candidate they support. But when you ask them what their foundational political/ethical philosophy is, they begin to squirm and fidget. Well...they really don't know, and they don't know because they haven't thought about it. You see, this is what we're talking about. Forget this nonsense that tells you what you believe – your values as we say (and not accurately, but that's a discussion for another day) – is no big deal, that it's all private anyway. That's the anti-theoretical lie of the modern West. You, me, and everyone else in all of creation are the product of what we believe. Thought precedes and guides action. Always. Another way of seeing it is that under stress you will not do something you haven't mastered through practice and your practice – or lack thereof – is the result of your theory... your beliefs.

We need to come right out and state it plainly. I'm not asking for your body alone and if you intend to give only your body – trying merely to pick up a few moves here or there, without committing to the core principles – Wing Chun will be next to useless for you and maybe even worse than that. This is the problem. I'm asking that you devote your mind and your body to this study (and every other that you're involved with, for that matter). Live a life fully engaged. Test everything and see if it makes sense. I believe that it does and that it forms a full and non-contradictory whole. These principles and the practices they give birth to are either true or they are false. I ask that you investigate them with the full power of your faculty of reason and, in so doing, you will arrive at two wonderful truths.

The first will be that you will see for yourself that Wing Chun is indeed a logical method of true hand-to-hand, life-or-death, all-or-nothing combat - a true self-defense system for this and any age. You will see that it's non-contradictory both externally and internally. Externally in that it's coherent with the facts of reality. You can use Wing Chun on a stairwell, in a parking lot or even in a pool – anywhere a true fight (we're not talking about competitive matches) takes place. Can you use Brazilian Jujitsu in a pool? Can you pull guard under water? You may say that the BJJ student may still use his skills in such an event by adapting to the environment of the pool or the stairwell, but you're mistaken. Such isn't an adaptation but a repudiation. He may be successful, but his success depends, in such circumstances, upon his ability *not* to use his primary discipline. This is what I mean when I say that Wing Chun is externally non-contradictory. Its concepts and applications can be used in any environment where there is an honest-to-goodness fight (not a match). And, naturally, it isn't internally inconsistent either. There's a logical progression to all the training (when taught properly) that will leave the student greatly confident, not scratching his head over the disparate nature of the educational chaos.

The second truth is that such a concept-based approach will allow the student to make Wing Chun work for them. The great Wong Shun Leung was fond of telling his pupils to make Wing Chun their slave, not to become its slave. This is the height of liberation and it may, at this point, intimidate you but I assure you that if you put your mind and body into it, not holding back from the hard work, you will master it. It's a system designed to be applied uniquely by individuals, not mass produced and applied by robots.

Okay...that's my rant on philosophy. If I've turned you off, I certainly won't apologize. In either event, please think deeply about these forthcoming truths and when I say deeply, I mean logically.

And remember, everything has to be applied in a real fight against a non-cooperative opponent. Never forget that. Your life and health depend upon it. This is no game. This isn't about whether you're the best student at your school. This is about fighting – life and death, safety or injury. In a real violent encounter, you don't get points for how good your form was, who your instructor is, or anything like that. You are either prepared for the speed and power of real-life fighting or you're not. This is what Wing Chun is; it's a fighting philosophy and method. And a combat philosophy is the purest of all philosophies because contradiction can get you killed straight away. So, if you're like me and you demand truth in everything you do, Wing Chun is for you. Read on and be amazed at this simple, yet comprehensive system. I've been studying it for nearly 40 years now and trust my life with it in a violent encounter and that's why I'm extending it to you for your consideration. I have no intention of this material helping you win tournaments, boxing matches or MMA fights. For those of us that understand the system, there's an undeniable beauty to it, but for the most part, Wing Chun is the Glock of fighting systems. Let other methods dazzle. Wing Chun has no intent to make you look cool. Its sole purpose is the preservation of your life and safety should you need it. That's it.

9

THE FOUNDATION
SIL LIM TAO

In a day and age where we routinely dismiss the past, telling modern warriors to learn and adhere to a weird looking little form seems to be an easy way to lose customers. Many people, as we've just discussed, want merely to learn a technique or two and not bother with training. They ask, "what should I do if this happens…or that?"

So, to begin their training with a form that doesn't directly address a specific problem immediately strikes people as fantastically odd. But, think about it: right now – as you read this – you're the product of what you've been practicing for the last few years. That's right. You, me...everyone...are a product of our discipline – or, in some cases, our lack thereof. Can you drive a car? It's because you've practiced in the past. Can you play the piano? It's because you went through the difficult process of learning to play it.

In short, there are too many variables to a simple question like, "what should I do if a guy throws a punch at me?" Which guy? Even if we narrow down the punch to a right-cross, we have multiple angles it can arrive due to the attacker's height, individual style, etc. Also, what else is happening? Are you in a parking lot, a stairwell, or blocking the front door to your house while your family is inside? You see, a simple question about a punch, when seen logically, isn't quite so simple anymore. So - and I know I'm repeating myself, but I think it's necessary on this point - you aren't going to get a proper self-defense method like you would buy a new shirt. You're going to have to work at it.

But, trust me, it's really worth it. All good things in life are, right?

With that said, Wing Chun's approach is to systematically make you into a weapon. That's the goal of any true martial art training. You personally become a highly sophisticated weapon full of tested combat reflexes and non-contradictory tactical and technical skills designed to be used in the event of a sudden violent encounter, anywhere, anytime. And Wing Chun begins making you into that weapon by teaching you its first form, Sil Lim Tao. The loose translation of this into English is "little idea" or "young idea." Basically, it's an ingenious library of fistic concepts and techniques. Practiced carefully and routinely, it will serve both as the foundation through which you will grow into the aforementioned weapon and as the signpost for application and training. In light of this, the rest of this book will seek to impart the core concepts of the SLT form since they set forth the key tactical and technical principles of everything Wing Chun seeks to accomplish in fighting.

You see, the modern approach is perfectly devoid of theory yet without proper theory, practice is blind and ignorant. Both the mind and the body must be honed into the weapon. What I'm putting forward, therefore, isn't a new way of doing Wing Chun, though some accuse me of doing that, but of the principled method of the Wing Chun concept. And it's this that's most important: to understand the core concepts of the philosophy and science of Wing Chun or else the techniques are applied blindly, in a vacuum. A thousand errors can be avoided if we stick to the nucleus and expand from there, always careful to go back and check our applications against core theories. This will keep us from being both a blind slave to movements we don't quite understand and from wandering so far afield that we aren't doing Wing Chun anymore.

The thing to know is that every mistake in Wing Chun can be traced back to an error in one of the first four sections of SLT. That's right. Just about every single Wing Chun mistake is a misapplication or misunderstanding of the form's initial four sections. This is the case because it's in these opening sequences that the system's core concepts are conveyed. Without understanding these core concepts, the Wing Chun fighter is blind; they're practicing movements devoid of conceptual/tactical guidance. The theologian Cornelius Van Til, as I mentioned earlier, used to say that there's no such thing as a brute fact...which is to say, there's no fact that's on a metaphysical island. The same goes with technique too. A thousand errors can be avoided when we comprehend and practice the core concepts of the SLT form.

The goal of our training should always be integration and reality. It's quite easy to focus merely on a few points and miss the larger picture, however. To inoculate us from doing this – from becoming too beholden to a minor rather than a major – we need to be careful students of the lessons of the SLT form.

Let's set down a few key points before we dive into the form, though.

The Main Thing

A great deal of confusion can be avoided when we start with a proper understanding of what Wing Chun is meant to accomplish for us and, just as importantly, what it isn't.

First, it's a self-defense system. This is to say that its highest goal is to give us a logical path to preserving our health and safety in the horrible event of an attack. All other goals – such as punching or kicking someone – are subordinate to this first one. The chief aim is for the student, in the event of a fight, to preserve as much of their safety, or the safety of loved ones, as possible. This differs tremendously from the primary goal of combat sport. Wing Chun's goal is not and never can be "winning" a fight that is voluntary – or, in other words, a match. Once a man or woman concedes to a match type fight, climbs into a ring or cage, for whatever reason, he or she has abandoned the primary goal of self-defense. In the immortal words of Dalton in *Roadhouse,* "No one ever wins a fight." In any altercation there are potentially horrible consequences. Many people lose their lives every year from taking a blow and then falling and striking their head on a hard surface. This often happens, as you see in the news reports, because one, two or more knuckleheads couldn't control their egos and tempers.

An example of just this happened recently in my hometown of Greenville, South Carolina. A gentleman had just gone out to eat with his wife and was leaving a restaurant when he became angry with another patron who was blocking his car in the parking lot. As it went, the gentleman was trying to pull out of his parking spot while another car was waiting for someone else to back out so that he could pull in. Well, this caused the gentleman in question – who was apparently around 60-years old, by the way – to grow rather angry. Words were exchanged. Horns were honked. The young man trying to pull into a spot apparently flipped the older man the New York state bird (that's an obscene hand gesture for those of you who live in pacifist areas like Amish communities...and Canada). The older man, now completely enraged, exited his vehicle and tried to remove the bird flipping, car blocking, ready-to-dine younger man from his car. Punches were thrown. In the melee, the older man was struck by a wild haymaker on the chin. Down he went. His head slapped hard against the unforgiving pavement.

There aren't mats out there in the real world.

He died.

He died because he couldn't pull out of his parking spot as fast as he preferred.

His wife was with him. She watched the whole affair. She saw him die. She lost her husband. Dead. Gone. And she lost him not to war, disease, old age, or anything like that. She lost him because of a temper tantrum.

There was an episode in the bathroom at a San Francisco 49ers game where some poor soul ended up, not dead, but brain damaged from his punch-induced swoon to the hard floor. Now, one can expect 49er fans to be a tad depressed, even irritated, considering how their team has been performing these past few years. That's unfortunate. But to nearly kill a man who's at the game with his family because you're mad about the jersey he's wearing (that's the allegation) is insane. So, anyway, you get the point. Fights often have unexpected consequences. Avoid fights whenever you can.

The surest way to stay safe is to never have to use your Wing Chun. Please remember that by training in a martial art you're in no way obligated to expose yourself to danger – or to ignore a chance to exit a violent scenario because, hey…you know how to fight. In point of fact, if you really know how to fight, you know how dangerous it is, how unpredictable it is, and how no good outcome can ever come from violence. A man or woman who successfully defends themselves, after all, has gained nothing. They only have what they already possessed and very likely, even in the event of a *victory*, have lost something.

Imagine the following:

Stockbroker dude (SD): Hey, man. Have I told you about this awesome new investment?
   You: No. What?
   SD: It's incredible! Superlative! Magnificent! Phenomenal! Astonishing!
   You: Dude…
   SD: Sorry. I was an English major. Naturally, I couldn't get a job, though.
   You: Oh. That explains it.
   SD: Luckily, there was finance.
   You: I understand.
   SD: Anyway, this is a once in a lifetime opportunity.

You: What's it gonna cost?

SD: Everything you've got. Your house. Your car. Your savings. Everything.

You: Seriously? I could lose everything?

SD: Yep. Isn't that fantastic?

You: (scratching your head) I don't know, dude. What's the upside?

SD: Nothing! You get to keep your stuff.

You: Have you taken any major blows to the head recently?

SD: Huh? No. Why?

Sure. It's fun. Wing Chun is a really cool and unique system that's exhilarating to train. That's true. But we should never, never forget the basis of what we're talking about. In a real fight, you have everything to lose and absolutely nothing to gain.

It's not a fair fight

Many people are shocked by the graphic nature of the art. But, remember, just because you aren't comfortable with something doesn't mean it isn't true. A fight is an ugly affair and Wing Chun makes no apologies for that reality. Moreover, it's always reality that gets the last laugh. In regard to fighting, reality says "Get real or get gone. It's truth or death...or, at least, serious injury."

If this causes you to shy away that's only because you haven't been fully honest about the previous point. This is no game. Boxing is a game – a rough game, but a game nevertheless. An all-out fight is no such thing and that's exactly why I've labored to point out that we must have a full and true understanding of what it is we're talking about here. When we do, and when we're true warriors, we will value peace and respect and love in such a way that causes us to live our lives in humble but strong honor. And we'll live by a code of such honor that will give no person offense so that if we're ever forced to fight we'll have full moral clarity in which to engage our threat.

Once engaged, however, and once forced to fight because retreat or de-escalation isn't possible, we must use everything at our disposal in which to defeat that threat. To hold back once the battle is joined is illogical and immoral in that any half-effort that allows the enemy to persist is an effort that puts you and/or your loved ones in more jeopardy. Wing Chun, therefore, isn't a system of half-measures or rules and it cannot function properly when limited by rules for the very reason that its very structure is designed to attack and defend the body's weak links. To take eye-gouges and throat strikes from Wing Chun is like forcing a marathon runner into a pool to race in a swim meet and saying, "...see, he's not a good athlete." Right from the get-go we're assuming that we must attack the other fellow's weak spots and protect our own. Does this mean that we don't spar? Of course, we spar. But sparring is a drill designed to enhance timing and distance control, etc. Wing Chun never assumes that sparring is a real fight; it uses boxing type drills but that doesn't mean Wing Chun fighters try and become boxers.

One common objection is easy to clear up and should be addressed. What of people who complain that using eye-gouges, throat attacks and knee kicks are unwarranted in "fender-bender" fights? What of people who say that using such tactics is an unneeded escalation and that in many altercations, less force can be used?

These questions and others like them betray our first principle. Rule number one for any true warrior is to always avoid violent confrontation so much as humanly possible. We must endeavor to live a life of such honor and integrity so as to greatly reduce the likelihood of anyone ever attacking us because of our own actions and/or words. I suppose there are scenarios where a quick punch, kick or shove might end an altercation with little damage but this is a dangerous thought process because, once an engagement begins, as we've seen, there's never a way to know how far it will go. What if you just punch a guy who's bothering you, running his mouth or something, and then he pulls a weapon? Or maybe he has some friends who think it's you who deserves a beating?

You see, a full and robust understanding of point number one – of keeping your safety the main thing – means that you'd most certainly be able to avoid or escape a "fender-bender" fight.

There's something else too.

When I was in middle-school, there was a kid that I picked on. I'd never been able to pick on anyone before that but had been learning self-defense, working out, and growing up so I found myself suddenly on the other side of things. Instead of being bullied, I became a bully – and trust me, it embarrasses me to this day to admit this. Anyway, I guess I'd been giving this kid (I still remember his name but will omit it for obvious reasons) the business a little too much. I passed him on my way back to my seat in class. He was sitting in a chair, reading. I said, "How ya doing, fat boy?" This was bad enough but along with my big mouth, I smacked him on the side of the head – kind of a wrap like you'd pat someone on the shoulder with, except I did it to his head. I kept walking. Suddenly I heard a commotion from behind me, saw the shocked expressions of fellow classmates, and turned to see what was going on.

Well, he walloped me with a haymaker.

You know...what I remember the most was the expression of indignation and shame on his face. He'd had it with me and that was it. He threw everything he had into that punch. The thing is, though, he was much smaller than I was and not very quick. He kept swinging wildly but I caught him in a head-and-arm and took him down. Once I had him under control I didn't hit him – just held him until the teachers came to break the fight up. We were marched to the Dean's office straightaway.

"What happened? How'd it start?" The Dean demanded, with us sitting in separate chairs in front of his desk. I was dabbing a tissue on my nose because it was still bleeding from the shock of the haymaker.

"I started it," I said. "It was my fault. I did it."

The Dean looked at me with surprise and so did the other boy.

"I was being a jerk, really hassling him and he got fed up. I deserved it. Send me to detention, not him."

The Dean studied both of us for a minute. The other boy sat there looking somewhat freaked out. His anger having waned, he looked frightened.

I turned to him and said, "Seriously. It was my fault. I deserved to get punched. No hard feelings. I'm sorry."

He was shocked and I think he may have started to cry a little but he caught himself and nodded.

The Dean watched us some more and asked me, "You sure that's it?"

"Yep," I replied.

"There's not gonna be a retaliation in the hallway later, is there?"

"No, sir."

He told the other boy he could go back to class. When we were alone he told me that he was both disappointed and proud of me at the same time.

"I'll go to detention," I said, "can you please just not tell my parents why?"

Well, not only did he not tell my parents what a knucklehead I'd been, he didn't even send me to detention. He kept me in the office until the class was over and then sent me on my way. "I can see you truly learned a lesson, son," he said. And I truly had. To this day I can still see that horrible look of shame on his face that I'd induced by my behavior.

I never repeated that behavior again.

The point of the story is that the only reason I was in a "fender-bender" fight was because I started the whole thing. If I hadn't antagonized the poor kid, none of that ever would have happened. You see, people rarely start fights with someone they think can beat the crap out of them. It's rare to hear a news story like this:

"Last night Mike Tyson was walking down the road and a local middle school student thought, 'hey, that's Tyson...I bet he can beat the crap out of

me.' The young man sucker punched the former heavyweight champion of the world, which, naturally, didn't faze the famed fighter. Then, a little irritated, Tyson unleashed a volley of blows, which all struck the deluded teenager like he was a pimple-laden heavy bag. Police are still trying to find all of the boy's body parts. After coming out of his coma, the young man told police that Tyson's reputation for power and speed are quite well deserved."

So, you see, that was sort of a fender-bender fight. All I needed was the clinch and aforementioned head-and-arm takedown. The thing is, though, the reason I only needed to use such limited technique, and was in so little danger, was that I STARTED THE FIGHT. I can't stress this enough – Wing Chun isn't meant for mutual combat any more than guns and knives are. If you forget this, you'll turn it into a competitive training method rather than a self-defense method. It's the difference between firing your handgun at a paper target and being in a real gunfight. In a real gunfight I don't want my enemy to get any shots off at all. Likewise, in a real hand-to-hand combat scenario, I want to use every single means possible to damage my enemy's ability to do me harm. Eye-gouging, knee stomping, throat striking, groin hitting, etc., they're all on the table (and specifically trained aspects of the system) or else you aren't doing a true combat system. You're training for a game.

So, let me be even more clear.

Wing Chun doesn't work against sport martial arts for the same reason a sniper doesn't win quick-draw competitions. Your goal with Wing Chun is to scientifically assault, in the most logically consistent manner possible your enemy's weakest links. That's it. Period. If you're doing it for any other reason, you aren't doing it for *martial art*. You've got a violent and cool hobby, that's all.

Wing Chun is ugly because real-world violence is ugly. That's just the way it is. As we like to say: it's not designed for you to look good but to make sure you still look good **after** the fight.

10

THE FOUNDATION'S FOUNDATION

THE YI JI KIM YUNG MA

I'm not going to make any apologies for both the look and the feel of this weird little stance. When I first came upon it over 30 years ago I wasn't pleased with it either. Pointing your toes and knees inward as you push your pelvis forward is no way to feel or look cool, that's for certain. But, remember, Wing Chun's goal is to keep us good looking after a fight – not before or during. Therefore, I'll come right out and say it: you're likely going to hate standing like this for long periods of time. It's as uncomfortable as it is bizarre in appearance. You aren't going to impress the ladies with this, trust me.

That said, let's address the importance of it and what it's helping you achieve.

Mobile Stability

We've already discussed how the environment you're fighting in is often as dangerous as the person you're fighting. The Wing Chun fighter, therefore, needs not only mobility, but also a mobility that can quickly offer "rooted" support to both drive through an opponent and have enough base to avoid being easily driven back. We must repeat that getting driven backwards is a serious problem in all-out fighting and the Yi Ji Kim Yung Ma (YJKYM) is the solution to this and a host of other perils.

The very name of the stance explains much. It means, basically, *character two goat gripping horse – or character two goat gripping stance.*

In Chinese the number two is a short line and a long line, which in regard to the YJKYM, can also be represented in the short line between the knees and the longer line of the heels. In other words, they're saying that this looks like their number two. It's simply a reference to the fact that the pinched in knees and the flared-out heels look something like their "character for the number two."

The goat gripping can cause some chuckles amongst those of us who haven't been on a farm for a few generations. That's understandable. If I had to get my food from a source other than a restaurant or refrigerator, I'd probably die within a week. But if you've ridden a horse or done any skiing you know well the feeling of having to pinch your knees in so that you maintain your balance. Also, if you watch baseball, you'll notice how many batters assume this very stance once in the box. They use it to "load" their body to stride toward the ball. This is an important point that's sadly missed in much of Wing Chun. Modern baseball players get paid millions and millions of dollars to play a sport and many of them use either the exact same configuration or a very similar one as the YJKYM uses to store energy through the pinching of the knees. This screams volumes of information at us.

First, it tells us that Wing Chun is interested in power generation using the whole body. Watch a baseball player get in the batter's box and get set. It's a very, very particular science for each player, though it varies a bit for everyone. The very best hitters – especially the home-run hitters – are currently getting paid north of $20 million a year, so their hitting approach is quite meticulous. Naturally, they want to hit the ball as solidly, and with as much stored energy (momentum), as humanly possible. Well, that's not unlike what you're getting ready to do in Wing Chun too.

The pinching in of the knees literally allows you to harness the body's energy while simultaneously keeping balance. Unlike a baseball player, though, the fighter doesn't know when the pitch is coming, and must be able to move freely in any direction at any time. The YJKYM, therefore, is a brilliant and scientific starting point to help us get the foundation right. Part of the foundation, though, is power. Remember that as you stand there feeling all weird and awkward. You're training for maximum power generation…eventually. (We'll cover the topic of hitting power in full detail in a future volume on the second form, by the way.)

The YJKYM works to retrain our nervous system. It forms the

basis of all our later footwork and kicking, in fact. But Wing Chun footwork is a close-range type of footwork. I know I'm going to repeat myself on this point time and again and that can be frowned upon, but the issue is so important that I'd rather irritate the reader then leave them under-informed on this all-important aspect. The YJKYM literally trains one's nervous system to get ready to move properly in a fight. If you use Muhammed Ali style bouncing footwork you're liable to get tackled and/or driven back. Wing Chun's goal is superior mobility *and* stability.

The hips are pulled forward as well, forming a "locked-in" lower body effect. It's a catastrophic mistake to apply this verbatim in fighting, however. The hips are forward and locked under you in order to train you for proper power generation. This is a technical training stance, not a tactical application principle. As mentioned before, the baseball player is not – repeat not – in their loading position when they hit the ball. They simply used the loading position to, well, load. It's the same for us.

A great many mistakes in Wing Chun can be avoided right here and now. To keep your hips locked forward at all times in combat is not the point. The issue at hand is training to load the stance and provide the proper neurological structure for everything to come. *The Wing Chun fighter is not to use this for their fighting principle any more than they are to keep their hands pulled back in the chambered position.* The hands are chambered to assist us in the habit of not turning our shoulders unwittingly. No one suggests that this is how they are to face an enemy – hands pulled back – so why the insistence on the hyper-literalism of the lower-body?

No. It trains power development. The YJKYM is not a fighting-stance – it's a training-stance.

11

CENTERLINE & CENTER OF MASS
SOFT TARGETS

There's a Time and a Season...

The second action of the SLT form is arguably the most misunderstood in all of Wing Chun. Often times it's taught as an example of two low *guan-sao's* and then two crossing *tan-sao's*. This is a perplexing bit of business in that neither technique has anything in the world to do with the actions here. For example, a *tan-sao* is a spreading action and a *gaun-sao* is a splitting action. Pushing the hands across your centerline – low, then high – is in no wise either a splitting or spreading action so one wonders how this erroneous definition came about. In short, it's likely because – lacking a tactical understanding of the purpose of the form – many were reduced to grasping at straws for an explanation of this odd action, which constitutes the initial hand motions of the entire system. It's so strange for an allegedly practical and logical fighting system to come out crossing its hands right at the get-go that many people are left confounded and mystified.

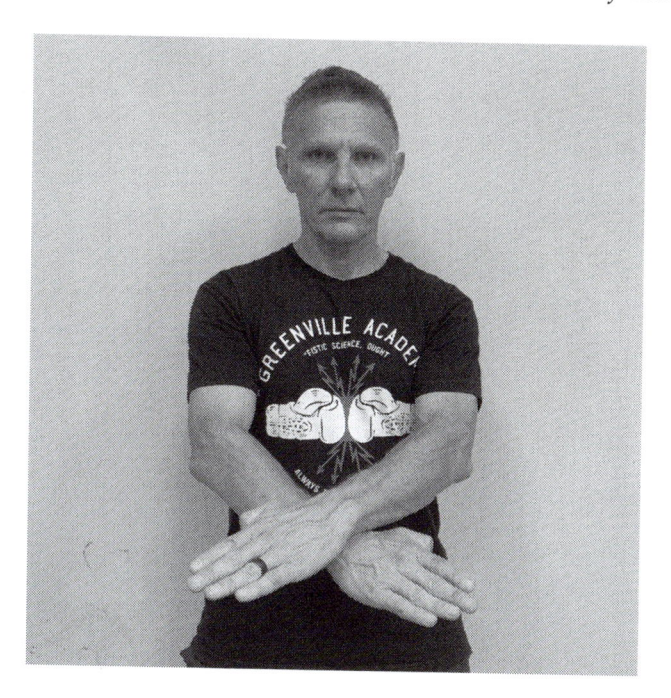

But the motions end in positions that one could, with some imagination, conclude are those aforementioned techniques. This beats just admitting that you have no clue.

The truth, however, is that we're going with tactical/technical principles in the form. We're building ourselves into the weapon to be used before we worry about the specifics. This makes the crossing of the hands – great sins in all-out fighting, I assure you – understandable.

Firstly, we're establishing the concept of "facing" (*chui-ying*). This is to say that in normal close-range fighting circumstances we don't want to "blade-off" or favor one side over the other. Wing Chun is firmly insistent upon this principle for the simple reason that when in close-range combat, in less than safe environments, one must be able to face their opponent fully so that they have:

1. Equal access to both sides so that one arm is never a "short" arm

2. Equal access to both sides so that all limbs can attack, defend and control
3. Full use of both upper body limbs in order to adequately deal with pushing/grappling style attacks (to blade off in close range puts you in a position where you can be easily flanked and/or overpowered
4. Maximum power. Imagine trying to bench press in a bladed position. Impossible.
5. The ability to move in any direction while not losing your facing position. This requires using the *chui-ying* concept at the outset

Imagine getting into a fight on a stairwell landing. In such an event an opponent might try to overpower you and cast you down the stairs, which could prove rather deleterious to your well-being. In the very least, it might make your insurance deductible go up. Or, imagine an opponent trying to push you off a sidewalk (into traffic perhaps) or hiking trail (over a cliff). Any of these scenarios is potentially catastrophic. Wing Chun rightly recognizes the horrible danger of falling in a fight by not only training us in a stable and mobile stance, but by making sure we're squared to our enemy. There's very little hope of stopping a hard push or rush or grab with only one side available. Remember, no one performs bench-presses (or any lift for that matter) with one side forward.

12

FACING

He who controls the position & angle controls the fight

The flip side of the facing coin is the concept of non-facing (*by-ying*). Simply put, a Wing Chun fighter, building on the footwork concepts already introduced – of rooted mobility, staying low and fast – endeavors to never let their enemy face them directly. Think about it: if directly facing your enemy helps you, it only makes sense to deny him the same privilege. To do this, of course, requires footwork and more footwork. That's why the SLT form opened with the YJKYM.

The facing/non-facing principle subsumes the concept of timing. A great fencing master was once asked which came first – timing or distance. His reply was classic. He said that such distinctions were for the philosopher to decide but the fencer had to perceive and act upon both at once. Both are of equal necessity.

A grave, grave error in all of martial arts – not just my beloved Wing Chun – is the attempt to use technique to solve a problem rather than to use timing and position. This is the key to understanding the facing/not-facing principle. Think about this: if a man is standing straight in front of you, he has multiple angles through which he might attack. Just looking at hand strikes, he might throw a right or left cross – and these might come from two or three different angles each! Or he could throw hooks, or curving uppercuts, straight uppercuts, or overhands. In all, if an opponent launches an attack dead-on, you likely have 8-10 different angles to cover – and quickly! This is not to mention combinations. After all, people rarely throw a single punch at you and then pause to see how you dealt with it. *"Ah... I see you've used an outward blocking action against my hook punch. Good for you! Now let's see how you deal with my famed overhand."* Such is the stuff of fantasy. A real fighter will launch multiple strikes...if he can.

By getting out of the traffic lane, Aaron has achieved a safer position from which to counter-attack. Should Josh follow with a right-hand swing, Aaron has the better angle and is ready for it. Good footwork is "offensively-defensive" or "defensively-offensive."

Would you play a game where you have to guess a number in my head 1-10 and if you miss I get to slap you as hard as I can? (If this sounds like fun, put this book down and go for therapy right now... and stop voting...and don't have children). Well, it's the height of folly to stand straight in front of an attack and try and pick it off when you have better, safer, more logical options.

The facing concept, however, correctly understood, teaches us to use footwork and/or shifting to create advantageous angles for attack and defense. Many get stuck on using simultaneous attack and defense techniques while leaving their feet planted – staying right in front of the attacker. But such is a drill for the classroom. A quick side-step by the Wing Chun fighter will render an attack ineffective and, moreover, will provide superior positioning for the follow-up. If your opponent can't face you directly and you're facing him, any attack he launches has to come from one direction[1]. Think about that for a moment and see what an advantage it gives you. If you successfully angle on your enemy, his next attack must come from one single angle rather than eight to ten. This makes you 8-10 times faster than if your enemy was able to directly face you! You've heard that speed kills – well, it does, and it will kill you if you're dumb enough to help your opponent by staying right in front of him.

What about the stop-hit, though? Is this to say that moving is better than simply using a counterattack right at the outset? No. The facing/not-facing principle subsumes the stop-hit policy still to come in that it preaches the supremacy of timing-position as a single unit of fighting importance. Clearly, it's always preferable to simply nail the bad guy with a stop-hit before he's able to attack. But this is dependent upon and, therefore, in service to, good positioning and timing. Once again, there is no good timing with bad positioning or good position with bad timing. Timing and position are co-equals, mutually dependent upon one another. Before any technique can be considered, one must have a solid and mobile base through which to achieve a superior angle to accurately score a blow.

.

The Necessity and Danger of Drills

If you were to join the Marines, you'd be shipped off for basic training. On my side of America, you'd go to Parris Island, South Carolina.

Once there, you would commence a round-the-clock immersion into what you need to do to become a United States Marine.

This is instructive for the Wing Chun fighter because the Marine is training for war and the self-defender is training for all-out combat, i.e., civilian self-defense. These two disciplines have a few things in common over against sport-based training.

For one, a boxer or MMA fighter has the distinct advantage of being able to test their training in a one-to-one environment. That's to say that to test their boxing, a boxer can engage in high-intensity boxing (hard sparring) or a sanctioned match. The Marine DI's can't, on the other hand, literally start shooting at their recruits. Wing Chun has the same limitation of combat training. A direct one-to-one test is too dangerous (not to mention illegal) to be uniformly applied to trainees.

European fencers died by the thousands in the Middle Ages until safe training practices were established – and that's precisely when there was real advancement in skill. You see, when people have to be seriously injured or killed to learn of their weaknesses, progress is rather restrained. The military has, therefore, developed entire training regiments based on these truths. They want the troops combat ready and they've isolated certain principles, habits and attitudes that need to be trained in order to achieve this goal.

So, the Wing Chun fighter, being unable to consistently test their theories against the reality they're training for, must do the same thing.

In any activity, and self-defense is certainly no exception, there is a necessity for drills in order to achieve optimum muscle memory and execution skill. Drills are isolation skill exercises. They limit the scope of an engagement or activity to hone in on the one or two things the trainee is trying to develop and/or enhance. Drilling is both proper and necessary for the student to achieve skill in his/her discipline.

The problem for self-defenders is that we can't train exactly as we'd have to perform since a real self-defense scenario has so many variables. The ideal would be for the student to be able to periodically engage in a fight, right? Of course, that's immoral, illegal, and horribly dangerous[2]. This fact makes logical drilling an absolute necessity for the Wing Chun fighter.

A drill should be as little removed from the action we're training for as possible while still being safe. For example, Marines shoot at targets, not each other. All drills should be as simple and direct to the point as possible. The more complex they become, the more they deviate time, energy and focus away from the simple brutality required in true fighting. Simple is always best. Full power and speed is the goal but this can only be gained through slower, less intense repetitions done properly over time (kung-fu means skill gained through time and work, after all).

So, how do we prepare ourselves for the intensity, fear and confusion of a real encounter since we can't practice it directly? Well, again, that's where military training lends us a hand.

The student must learn how to deal with pressure – both physically and emotionally. One of my favorite pieces of entertainment is watching movies that include tough Drill Instructors picking on recruits. Some of the things these guys say are flat-out hilarious. The thing to remember, though, is that it's all done with a goal in mind. They aren't being super rude to vulnerable men and women just because they can. They're doing it because they're preparing the soldier to deal with pressure. And pressure is always emotional! Never forget that. When things go wrong, we become emotional. Some of us might panic. Some of us might lose our temper. Others might freeze.

All of us are going to be impacted. We're all going to be impacted by the pressure of a violent encounter. When fear strikes, you will, indubitably, struggle with your emotions. And that's exactly why training soldiers for war routinely includes yelling at them, cursing at them, belittling them, and making them as uncomfortable as can be without being unsafe.

I grew up watching *Kung-Fu Theatre* on Saturday afternoons. My favorite movies always involved a tough – but funny – Sifu who trained his student hard. I loved the process. *The Karate Kid* came out in America in 1984 and introduced this unique relationship to mainstream audiences. When people saw it – and saw how the instructor took a young man who was weak and couldn't control his emotions – and through disciplined training, broke him down and then built him up into a man of strength and honor, they enrolled their kids in karate schools by the millions.

A problem arises, however, when this drilling is confused with the real thing.

You seldom see this in activities like boxing, MMA, football, etc. Because the participants get to engage in the activity they are being drilled for, it's rare for the drills to take on too much importance, thereby overshadowing the skill in performance the drill was intended to cultivate. For example, boxers work on speed bags and when they do they often have their chin up and they roll their hands one over the other. This would be a horrible way to fight but no boxer I know of has ever tried to hit a live opponent with such punches. The speed bag is there to help the trainee develop hand/eye coordination, looseness, and shoulder endurance (to keep their hands up during a fight). In the NFL many players practice explosiveness by doing plyometric exercises like jumping on a box from a stationary position. But, like in the boxing example, they know that jumping on a box is merely a means to an end.

In Wing Chun, though, there is an unfortunate tendency to confuse drills for fighting. Students spend vast amounts of time drilling in ways that – absent performance in fights or sparring – become more and more complex, which is to say removed from the reality of fighting. This is always a weakness for a martial art because sport-based skills can constantly be engaged in with relative safety – not to mention legality. You just can't get into fights all the time to test your martial art skills – even if you live in, say, Texas. This is a clear obstacle for anyone looking to become efficient at all-out fighting.

What has happened, therefore, is that Wing Chun has become far too smitten with exhibition style training. Too much flash and not enough footwork to keep the enemy out of position. Too much chi-sao where both parties are facing each other directly and not enough sparring and footwork drills where the trainee learns to avoid being an accessible target. Of course, chi-sao is an indispensable part of Wing Chun but it's merely a drill. To confuse it with fighting is dangerously silly. And, based off of the principles we've just covered, chi-sao should absolutely not be trained more than footwork because superior positioning is the key to combat success.

The facing/not-facing concept of Wing Chun, unlike some other aspects of the system, must be trained and drilled with great vigor since it is so vitally important to the success of the trainee in a real fight. Tragically, because so many students have never had this concept fully explained to them, they spend all of their time developing stationary fighting skills. This is like only firing your gun at the range – from a fixed position – and assuming from there that you will be perfectly accurate in a gun fight. But getting shot at is vastly different than shooting at a fixed target and the first rule of a gun fight is, after all, to not get shot. It's hard to be accurate when you're dead. Likewise, the logical street fighter seeks to be a hard target while at the same time being on the counter-offensive. The best defense is indeed a good offense – but we should take careful notice of the word *good*. For our purposes, and we'll cover this more in detail in the next section, our offense and our defense are an integrated whole. Fighting isn't American football where the one side is sitting on the bench drinking the refreshing beverage of their choice (note my assiduous efforts to avoid corporate sponsorship) while the other is playing. Both go. Both engage simultaneously. One must not compromise the other. And Wing Chun's first defensive goal is denial of a good target. This makes it less likely that we have to use actual defensive techniques like blocking.

The facing/not-facing principle demands that the Wing Chun fighter trains and drills for mobility.

The Danger of a Set Opponent

. . .

An enemy isn't dangerous because they are strong and fast. They're dangerous because they're set...they're ready.

How dangerous is the world's best fighter when he's sleeping? How dangerous is the world's greatest sniper when he doesn't have a gun? You see, the primary objective – above all else in self-defense fighting - is to shut-down your opponent's primary offensive weaponry. You have nothing to gain in a street fight and everything to lose. Obviously, outside of running or avoiding the threat altogether, a full defeat of the enemy is the best way to nullify their ability to carry an attack to you. But this can be taken to dangerous extremes.

For example, I've known countless Wing Chun men (and women) over the years that oversimplify – that is, they leave out relevant detail. Clearly, the best way to deal with a violent threat (once engaged) is with superior violence. No doubt. But the *chui-ying/by-ying* principle cautions us not to be reckless. Our first priority is to keep ourselves as safe as possible and defeating the enemy with a superior counter-attack is a corollary of this primary goal. If this can't be achieved without respect to the first point then our counter-attack must wait. No smart warrior exposes himself/herself recklessly. Great care, logic and training must go into the use of technique and tactics to simultaneously shut down the enemy attack while countering with our own.

This is a critical mindset to understand because human beings are not machines. You are always acting according to your deepest beliefs and convictions. Most people aren't very clear as to what those beliefs are – in fact, most of us are rather contradictory in many regards. Nevertheless, we must be clear on combat and its overriding goals. It's too easy to fall prey to sport thinking, which is to say that you operate under the premise that it's a match and you must win it. No. That's not true. You must shut down your enemy's ability to hurt or kill you. This is first. If this alone is done, yet you do no damage to him in the process, you have still "won" the fight.

Imagine for a second that terrorists attack your house one evening because you've been drawing pictures of a certain religious figure for a magazine. Not to offend anyone, but let's say you've been producing Buddha cartoons and a group of crazed Buddhists attack with AK-47's. They're all riled up and they're ready to go all seven paths of destruction upon your noggin. Well, being pacifist Buddhists, they probably don't have a clue how to fire an AK (or even a squirt gun for that matter) and they stand around chanting weird prayers in a foreign language as you scramble for your shotgun. Well, naturally, you realize that they aren't firing at you and so you just tell them to go away, which they do because all of this anger is exhausting them. Well, have you lost the fight because you didn't shoot, stab, kick or punch anyone? Some people would think so. They think the goal of self-defense is hurting the other guy but that's never the case. It's always, always, always, trying to protect what you already have. In this case you've done that, so you win.

This is a critical point. Ego makes many men think that they have to win the fight by bashing people into the ground. This is nonsense. Anger, fear and ego must be defeated – and this is a hard thing for many men. The proverbial, *"You don't know who you're messing with..."* may or may not be true but it's irrelevant to the extreme. A true warrior never, never engages in trash-talk before a battle unless there's something tactical to be gained – some psychological advantage perhaps. A true warrior keeps his emotions in check regardless of the circumstances. Thus, a true warrior, if combat is imminent, is busy seeking advantage. They aren't telling the bad guy how tough they are.

Such ego driven engagements lead one to ignore the facing concept and allows the enemy a good position to set up an attack. This leads to the conundrum of having your best technique – the straight assault – possibly coinciding with your enemy's best counter attack.

Many Wing Chun students love the chain punch attack. They reason that it's so wickedly fast and direct that no one has the ability to block that many punches. And they're right except that many fighters couldn't care less about Wing Chun structures and have no qualms about ducking and swinging or shooting for takedowns. In such events the Wing Chun attacker may very well run right into a nasty counter overhand punch, or an easy takedown.

These risks are heavily minimized, however, by using the facing concept. Quick, cat-like footwork will create angles that make counter-attacks much more difficult to come by. The greatest fighter in the world will have trouble if he can't reach you. If he's facing you directly, he should be just a tad too far away; if he can reach you, he shouldn't be able to face you or you should have control of his limbs and balance. This allows the Wing Chun fighter to *constantly* attack because his footwork and positioning are the tools through which he shuts down the enemy's offense. If there's anything that is most ignored or misunderstood in martial arts it is certainly this. The facing concept rests upon and proceeds from the foundation structure of the YJKYM and its attending footwork.

Franken-chun the Wing Chun Monster

By ignoring this all-important aspect of Wing Chun tactics, many students turn into a sort of Frankenstein monster – marching forward mindlessly with their arms extended in the Donnie Yen/Ip Man manner. They seem to think that in doing this there is a magic that will work for them and their foe will succumb to the great power of the superior force of the centerline. So, they march forward, their hands blocking the same line twice – and this line, of course, being a line that modern street fighters never attack. It's high minded foolishness. It's akin to WWI troops running at machine guns – trying to run faster than bullets (that didn't work too well, by the way). Or it's like the Boxer Rebellion. Or it's like getting into an argument with your wife. In any event, it's a horrible error of tactical thinking but it's not Wing Chun's fault. Rather, it's the fault of teachers training students in an incomplete version of the method. Wing Chun is logical and running head long at an opponent who is set is not logical. Wing Chun has great footwork – side steps and angle-steps and even retreating steps – that must be practiced and properly deployed to achieve maximum positional advantage in fighting. Plus, in the event that you can't overwhelm your enemy for whatever reason (perhaps he's a world-class athlete and you aren't) the chui-ying/by-ying concept can at least assist you in shutting down his attack despite your inability to totally end the threat.

13

BRING IN THE CALVARY

THE FOOTWORK OF WING CHUN

Now that we have a proper understanding of Wing Chun's basic stance, the YJKYM, and the facing/not-facing concept (*chui ying/by-ying*), it behooves us to look at the transportation system Wing Chun uses to facilitate superior positioning in a fight. We should go so far as to say that poor footwork is the single gravest error to commit in fighting with regard to technique. It's easy to do in Wing Chun because the hand techniques are, well, so cool, and you can easily fall into the trap of standing still and perfecting complex hand actions in a vacuum. But it's footwork that allows a fighter to dominate simply because the person that controls the angle and timing of any exchange is the one that has a clear advantage.

The core concept of applying the science of Wing Chun in a fight is that the best defense is a scientifically sound counter-attack. This is the heart and soul of Wing Chun. Don't play defense; attack the attack. This concept, however, can be dangerously over-simplified if we leave out the aforementioned principles like facing/not facing, which requires, naturally, the use of footwork and shifting. Countering an attack with one of your own without first having created a superior angle will naturally deteriorate into a slugging match.

==Therefore, the proper use of Wing Chun has the fighter moving and shifting in order to place his/her enemy at a disadvantage.==

Real fights don't often happen in optimal environments. A trained boxer, for example, has the advantage of ropes to safely hold him up should he/she be pushed backwards. An MMA fighter too has the help of a cage – not to mention the padded floor. Several years ago, I attended an MMA match in Charlotte, North Carolina when one of the fighters drove his opponent backward into the cage. This happens all the time in MMA – causing the fighters to smash into the cage and then they begin to grapple for position and/or exchange knees and elbows. Well, in this particular instance the fighters hit the cage door, which for some reason hadn't been properly closed. The result was that the two highly conditioned, well-trained fighters flew out of the cage when the door swung open – flying out of the sport world, as it were, and into the cold, merciless hands of reality.

You can imagine everyone's horror as the two young men, locked in combat a second before, burst out into the open and crashed to the cement floor several feet below them. We never did learn how badly they were injured but the fight was over at that point and both were taken to the hospital.

This instance is instructive to our point. Most martial arts today (we may even be so bold as to say all of them) do not diligently train with their environment in mind. The UFC has a motto – "as real as it gets" – that ignores not only foul tactics like groin and eye attacks but, more importantly, the environment they're fighting in. In real life, according to most reports, the vast majority of street fight injuries – serious ones – happen when one of the combatants strikes a fixed object like a counter top, table, or curb. This is exceedingly awful when it's the head that whacks into such an unforgiving surface. Also, many street fighters have suffered broken legs, ankles and feet because they've tripped or fallen off a step or sidewalk. In all, real fighting presents challenges to footwork that sport matches do not and it's here that Wing Chun offers perhaps its clearest advantage to the person seeking real-world, rather than sport based, fighting skills.

The YJKYM, as mentioned, forms the basis of one's footwork in that it teaches proper weight distribution and spring loading. Proper footwork must be *both quick and rooted*. Because of the potential to fall on uneven or slippery surfaces, good footwork must be shuffling in nature, not bouncing. And, most important, it must transport the fighter in a facing position lest they risk being overpowered and driven backwards. In short, the Wing Chun fighter seeks to be Tyson-like in their movement – rapid, smooth, explosive when needed, and still rooted (that is to say, with a low center of gravity).

14

THE VERSATILE YJKYM

To start moving we need a base to move or else footwork becomes bad dancing (of which I'm also a master, by the way). The base that you'll be moving is your YJKYM. That's right! The weird little stance that you've been working on (sometimes we call it the Sil Lim Tao stance) is actually the centerpiece of the whole fighting machine. This is precisely why the first form must be trained properly and repeatedly.

To get ready to move, simply lift up your toes in either direction and shift. To shift right, imagine that your left knee pushes the front of your right foot. Doing this properly will keep the same relationship between the knees and toes as you shift and avoid the "air" going out of your stance. When you do this, your hips should stay in place.

Once you've done this you have two options. You can keep your upper body facing forward, which leaves you in a diagonal-on stance, or you can turn the trunk to face an opponent. In the latter case, you'd have a leg forward but you'd still be directly facing the enemy. This is the wondrous versatility of the YJKYM. It gives you multiple options without a lot of fuss and also shows us the first – and, arguably, the most important link between the Wing Chun forms and actual fighting.

Incidentally, to call something a stance in Wing Chun is technically a misnomer since everything is done within the system to transport and deliver the weapons rather than to stand in a fortified position. Indeed, the very notion of a stance conjures in the mind an immovable person and nothing could be further from the truth of fighting and the science of Wing Chun. There's simply no way to remain immobile and safe at the same time as the human body is too vulnerable for such a plan. Flesh and bone do not make a good fortress.

We don't fight out of the direct YJKYM as it's inherently unstable. We must put one foot forward or shift the alignment in order to fight. If you remain forward facing during the shift you're in a diagonal-on position (a more formal name is the *Doi Gok Ma*). If you turn to face the enemy – either right or left – you're in the basic on-guard (or *Saam Gok Ma*). The on-guard looks quite like an old school boxing stance. To move forward or back in the latter stance, the Wing Chun fighter can merely step-and-slide – the forward foot going forward first, the back one catching up. To move back, the back foot moves first when retreating and then the front one shuffles after it. This is an easy procedure that can be done quite rapidly and with great structural force when in contact with the enemy.

The diagonal-on position is designed to face the potential or actual opponent without committing a full side forward, which keeps the Wing Chun fighter in a facing position and allows them to be ready to move quickly as the situation changes. One of the great tricks to the science of Wing Chun footwork is how simply it allows the transfer from one angle to the next by the subtle shifting of alignment. This allows the Wing Chun fighter the ability to move without actually having to move much at all. In my personal opinion, it's perhaps the greatest secret of the whole system (and it's a secret merely because most of us never bother to look at the footwork closely enough).

In many cases, the Wing Chun fighter can advance in the on-guard and quickly shift to a diagonal-on as the situation changes (such as the enemy moving or another fighter entering the fray). This is the lower body corollary of the facing concept. For us to use the facing concept properly in fighting, we must have ambidextrous footwork – thus, we have a leg forward (on-guard position) but not necessarily a side forward, which gives us the ability to change angles with amazing rapidity. This also allows the fighter to move about with tremendous economy of motion, which, so importantly, preserves energy. After all, once we're gassed, we're toast! Never forget that.

There are three great advantages to the diagonal-on stance, by the way. First, there is the great benefit of not having a leg forward that could be used as a target for the enemy's round kick or grappler's takedown. Secondly, the *Doi Gok Ma* doesn't appear to be a fighting stance, giving the Wing Chun fighter both the element of surprise and the quite critical look of a person who was *not in a fighting stance prior to the altercation*. In the heavily legalized West where a lawyer is likely lurking behind every bush, one has trouble claiming self-defense[1] if they consented to the fight. Mutual combat is against the law. This isn't a sparring match with two people stalking each other. Don't forget that.

Finally, the diagonal-on provides a highly scientific position from which to "negotiate" in a pre-fight scenario. We do well to consider that many assaults are simply not out of the blue; many are preceded by some type of verbal engagement. An attempt to deescalate should always made. It's madness (as well as immoral) to gladly enter into what could be a deadly altercation, so everyone is wise to work on their prefight skills and learn to talk their way out of trouble. But this must not be done from a position that telegraphs weakness. Many victims of sucker-punches make the mistake of trying to appear too cool in the face of danger and have their hands down – some even put their hands in their pockets while they're harangued and threatened. This is akin to dousing yourself in alcohol before trying to dash out of a burning building.

For a successful sucker punch to score (the attack method of men of low character far and wide) one needs two ingredients: a punch and a sucker. Don't be a sucker; have your hands up when engaged with a threat. Always. Always.

The goal is to achieve maximum balance of all considerations: moral, legal and tactical. A strong position that isn't a provocation is good and a neutral position that conceals your ability to quickly attack is even better[2].

The diagonal-on position, therefore, is perfect on these dual fronts. It creates a "fence" that discourages the sucker punch, showing the potential enemy that you won't be easily taken out by a haymaker and yet it doesn't appear too aggressive. You're ready for combat while not appearing to be the aggressor.

The diagonal-on is basically the position you end up in the *Yi-Bong* section (shifting Bong) of Wing Chun's second form, *Chum Kiu*. The difference, of course, is that instead of standing diagonal-on with a *Bong/Wu* guard, you have your hands up – alternating between the interview position (palms together…almost like you were praying) and the pleading position (palms forward, hands high and in front of the face). The transitions between these two should be practiced in class or in front of the mirror so that you get the hang of them and they become second nature to you. The goal is for you to appear neutral while fully ready to engage the enemy should it be necessary. Remember, appearing vulnerable invites violence but so does showing too much aggression. The diagonal-on position gives us the best of both worlds in such pre-fight predicaments.

The on-guard position will occur rather organically in the event of an altercation – depending upon your needs. We must point out this particular issue though: if you have the time and necessity to assume a full on-guard position prior to engagement, you've likely missed an opportunity to either escape or launch a preemptive counter-attack. Standing in an on-guard position and waiting for a fight to start is tactically unwarranted and legally suspicious. Honor and legality demand that we not wait around in an area where violence beckons. Our safety (and/or the safety of our loved ones) is the matter at hand. Leave the area, deescalate creatively if you can't leave, or attack if the previous options are not applicable for whatever reason.

15

FOOTWORK…LIKE CLOCKWORK

Good footwork doesn't mean movement for the sake of it. Good footwork isn't (necessarily) bouncing around like Muhammad Ali. It's the expeditious movement of your fighting arsenal; it's movement with the intent to deprive your enemy of a target and/or to provide the safest access to your enemy without violating the first goal. Fighters that lack quality footwork routinely end up "trading" shots, which is a clear violation of the facing/not facing principle and brings to mind the old Samurai maxim, "make sure your best attack doesn't coincide with your enemy's best counter."

All-out fighting, as we've discussed, is hardly ever fought on ideal footing. If it is, one naturally assumes that it's not a real fight but some kind of match set up between competitive fellows. And, just by way of reminder: a real fight is incredibly dangerous. A loss may include grave bodily injury or death. A victory might even include the same – but of the other fellow, which may result in you being in legal trouble. Always, always, always, avoid getting into a fight so much as it depends on you. If you absolutely must compete there's are very fine ways of doing that in disciplines like boxing, MMA and BJJ. Find a good coach and go for it.

Proper Wing Chun footwork, therefore, being logically consistent with the facts of reality, must train us to move in any/every direction as smoothly and rapidly – and with as much balance lest we get pushed or pulled off our base – as humanly possible. To answer the question that might come to mind in a moment – which step is the most important? – we answer without equivocation: the one you need right now!

Imagine that you're standing in the middle of a big clock, facing noon/midnight. Our goal is to be able to move to any hour on that clock, and then to another, and then another, without hesitation or loss of balance – and when we say balance, we mean the basic structural integrity of the YJKYM. Now, naturally, in the course of a fight, the enemy will be moving too, so the clock would, in effect, be changing directions with your movement so we're always considering this in terms of application but for the simplicity of presenting this material in book form (no easy task, thank you) let's keep things simple by assuming at first just ourselves, the footwork and the aforementioned clock.

Forward Shuffle

To move forward to the 12 o'clock line simply step either foot directly forward. Wing Chun is generally a rear-wheel drive system so the back foot will push you forward and then shuffle up behind the front. Another way of seeing the footwork of Wing Chun is that all steps are generally push-shuffle type steps – the back foot pushes both the body and the advancing foot forward and then shuffles up to join the fray. This can be done with or without a strike but one naturally assumes that the very reason to be moving forward is to engage the enemy.

The forward-shuffle can also be used to move anywhere along the forward line. If moving forward to your 10 o'clock to noon area, move the left leg first. The right leg goes first if moving in the other direction, from noon to 2 o'clock. This makes sure that you don't cross your feet. Like we said, when going directly forward, either foot can move first, but if going forward at an angle move only the left foot first when going from 10-12 and the right foot when going 12-2.

After you arrive at your destination you'll be in the on-guard position. You'll have one leg forward but not a side forward as you maintain a squared upper body relative to your target. Of course, if needed, you may turn your trunk slightly to the side in order to close off your body and/or extend the range of your punch or kick. Doing this isn't a sin[1].

As promised, you'll now see how integral the YJKYM is to your Wing Chun. To check the integrity of your footwork (check your math, really), simply lift up the front of your advance foot and turn the toes inward. Leave the rear foot in exactly the same position. When you do this you should be in your YJKYM! We call this the *"The YJKYM Check"* and it's absolutely vital in helping us develop proper footwork because good footwork is not – repeat not – simply moving your feet. Any knucklehead can move their feet. It's the proper movement of your base weaponry to a more serviceable and superior position relative to your opponent.

When you do the YJKYM-check you'll likely discover that your feet have drifted too far apart or too close. This is par for the course... just keep practicing. But don't ignore this problem because fighting will require rapid stepping and shifting and often times several quick, short steps in a row in a multitude of directions. The superiority of your Wing Chun will evaporate in short order if after one step you're off balance and can't move expeditiously to the next place. *I cannot stress this enough.* If you neglect this aspect of your training, your Wing Chun will be virtually useless, like a car with a great engine but a flat tire. Many Wing Chun trainees, enamored with the hand techniques, give no attention to the footwork and try to solve everything with a *sao*. This is like being in a gun fight and relying on your bullet proof vest to protect you instead of moving and getting cover. Go slow and develop good body feel and keep checking your footwork with this simple method and soon you'll be able to move with intuitive skill, balance and speed. Then you'll be a fighter! But not before. Never before.

Stepping back

To move backwards simply reverse the process. The same principles are in play – either foot can move directly to 6 o'clock but only the right should move towards 4 and left towards 8. To violate this principle will render your stance too narrow and make it much more difficult to project power as well as withstand an attack or push.

There are many people in Wing Chun that boldly proclaim that there's no retreating footwork in the system. But, as my Sifu once said, a car without reverse isn't a good car. Such talk is nothing but ignorant bravado. In real fights one must be able to move in *every* direction. Furthermore, Wing Chun is known as a "soft/hard" system that doesn't fight force with force. Why would I block a haymaker if I can let it miss me and then rush into the gap when the enemy is off-balance? The back-step (*Hua Ma*) is excellent against overhand swings and hooks precisely because momentum is dangerous. It's dangerous for you if you get caught by the haymaker and dangerous for the man throwing the punch if he misses since it carries him past the target.

Angle Steps

When in retreat it's advisable, whenever possible, to move back at a slight angle. Moving directly backwards, though sometimes necessary, is indeed dangerous because you're still directly in the line of the enemy. One simply cannot go backwards faster than forward. But turning side-to-side is another matter altogether and this is where angle-step and side-step come into play.

Technically, if you step backwards to 4 or 5 o'clock (moving the right leg first, of course) or to 7 or 8 o'clock, you are doing what's called a *Tui Ma*. You can classify this as an angled *Hua Ma* if you want...it doesn't matter what you call it, it matters that you can get where you need to go exactly when you need to get there! Basically, *Tui Ma* means pushed-step and it's the expert's retreat in that it gets you off the line of the attack while giving you a nice angle from which to counter-attack.

In the event of either of these, the front wheel now pushes the back wheel. If moving the right leg back, the left leg pushes and then shuffles into position afterwards. The upper body should maintain facing position throughout the movement and once again at completion the Wing Chun fighter is in the on-guard position. And just like with the forward footwork, the check can be done by pivoting the toes in to see if you have maintained the integrity of your YJKYM.

There are many versions of Wing Chun where a disproportionate amount of weight is placed on the rear leg, giving the fighter the look of a man fighting a hurricane force wind. Standing like this can come in pretty handy if, in fact, you live in the tropics and get into fights during Category 3 and above hurricanes. Besides that, though, it's highly illogical for a number of reasons and angling and retreating footwork are chief amongst them. If too much weight is placed on the rear leg, there will be no way to move backward quickly enough to avoid an attack. That some in Wing Chun reject this reason with the aforementioned proclamation that they never retreat in *true* Wing Chun is testimony to their lack of real world experience. And even if this was the case it still prohibits them from moving to the angle near the rear foot with anything resembling real speed. Proper weight distribution throughout should be roughly 50/50 with slight variations due to conditions. Placing more than 60% of the weight upon the rear foot at any time will render a fighter terribly immobile and fighting is about moving. The goal of a great Wing Chun fighter should be to be like water; a man with too much weight on his rear leg is more like a glacier.

The *Tui Ma* is certainly preferred to the *Hua Ma* but, even still, the *Hua Ma* is preferred to getting clobbered.

Side-Step

We've covered every direction on the clock except for straight side-steps (9 and 3). To do this is relatively easy. If you're moving to your three o'clock, push off the left foot and move the right in a direct line sideways. Reverse the order when going to your left. As always, move both feet equal distance so as not to spread your feet too far apart by accident or bring them too close together. Keep using the "YJKYM check" to assess your progress. This step – a middle step between the forward and angled movements – rounds out your ability to step in any direction at any time. A basic mistake to avoid: don't try and cover too much ground in a single step. It's better to use two or three rapid, but small steps, than one lunging step that will disrupt your balance.

The side-step, or *Cho Ma,* is an excellent step to use in conjunction with the forward-shuffle to facilitate an attack. It's so effective, in fact, it's precisely the footwork seen in the first section of the Wooden Dummy form (*Mook Yan Jong*) learned later in the system. A lightning quick – and short – step to the side (leaving you in the diagonal-on), followed by the forward-shuffle and an attack, is especially effective in fighting. In doing so, you will often be able to avoid your enemy's attack and, by virtue of the side-step, create a *chui ying-by ying* positional crisis for your foe as well. *This is an excellent example of how the Wing Chun fighter is constantly on the attack while at the same time not reckless.* Good footwork that moves the YJKYM and the striking tools to optimal tactical positions is what allows the Wing Chun fighter to be strongly aggressive without sacrificing their health in the process.

16

THE BEST BRIDGE TECHNIQUE
THE PUNCH

Ip Man was once asked what the best bridging technique was in Wing Chun. His answer might surprise you. The venerable grandmaster didn't say it was *pak-sao*, or *bong-sao*; in fact, he didn't mention a *sao* (hand) at all. Instead, he matter-of-factly replied that it was the straight punch to the nose. And a hearty AMEN to that!

After the opening of the YJKYM and the critical definition of centerline and facing, Wing Chun's ingenious first form gives us our first and primary weapon – the vertical fist punch. As noted previously, this volume doesn't intend to focus on the nuts and bolts of the physical structure (of which there is much good to say). We are, rather, exploring the often ignored or greatly misunderstood tactical/application aspects of the system. In this instance many ardent Wing Chunners are woefully misinformed and ignorant.

Let's understand that before we see the punch introduced it's built on the foundation of the mobile stance as well as the critical positioning principles of *chui ying/by ying*. As foundational as the straight punch is, it's utterly reckless to dash forward firing willy-nilly as you often see Wing Chun fighters do in videos. This is foolhardy because it leaves out relevant detail – specifically, gaining better positioning and timing through footwork before launching a serious attack. To be aggressive without regard for defense is the mark of the amateur.

Also, we note that we don't see the chain punch until the end of the form. This has been interpreted wrongly, we think. Since the chain punch finishes the form many posit that this punch isn't really a punch but some odd way of defining the vertical centerline. A good many Wing Chun people teach and think this – some quite qualified and distinguished in their own right. I respectfully and vehemently disagree with that assessment.

In the next section of SLT we have the introduction of the *fook-sao*, which is likened to a multi-tool without an attachment on the handle. The *fook* concept can be used for a variety of purposes so in the form the hand rests in that cupped position. The vertical fist punch, however, has no such issue. It's a knuckle sandwich. The fact that it's thrown only once, and then again in solo fashion with the right hand, does not, methinks, lower it from the realm of fighting technique – somewhere beneath the importance of the ubiquitous chain punch. Instead, it's a tactical/technical introduction of the concept of interception. A chain punch is more or less a finishing move – an attack on a secured line that has been opened by some mistake on our opponent's behalf, perhaps because of a miss, or by some smart action of our own. The straight punch, though, thrown once, or twice or even several times, is something short of a fully committed measure. It's like shooting while behind cover because the enemy still has ammo and is capable of shooting back at you.

In all, the straight punch reminds us of the supremacy of the simplest strokes in Wing Chun. And, like the YJKYM, there is more that this implies – namely the straight kick. Both weapons are used interchangeably depending upon range and need and neither should suffer from telegraphic movements.

It's true that to throw the punch in SLT we first bring the fist into the middle from the chambered position, but this is merely a matter of its use in the form. In a fight you wouldn't be carrying your hands on either side of your chest anyway, so this is to make sure that you move the punch in a straight path in front of your body. As long as I've been involved in martial arts, going back to 1981, I've never seen anyone throw a natural straight punch with the elbow down, driving a vertical fist forward. Never. Not once. This is the point in introducing Wing Chun's all-important workhorse this early in the form. It allows the student to very quickly get to work on delivering the punch correctly and making contact with the bottom three knuckles.

Here is a short list of some of the basic mistakes that the proper practice of the punch in SLT will help avoid and/or overcome. This can serve as an excellent example of how brilliant and logical Wing Chun is. We should remember that the forms are the foundational delivery system of the method's core concepts and structures. We may adjust our application of these concepts and structures in different eras and times but they're still the same – just our application needs change. Understanding this will allow each generation of students to gain the full counsel of the method. Something that may not work against one generation of fighters (because of style differences) or in a particular environment, may very well be needed again in the future. To properly pass along the system – and learn it – we must know and master the core concepts conveyed through the forms and important drills.

MISTAKE #1 – *Swinging*

Even when throwing a punch to a target straight in front of their nose, people will wing their elbow out. This, of course, causes telegraphic motion, which allows the enemy a better chance to see and react to the blow. Practicing the straight punch in the form makes one immediately aware of the elbow. The elbow should guide the punch and stay down during the delivery.

Most people don't know that the number one injury in boxing isn't to the face – nor the nose or eye. It's the hand that gets hurt. This happens with alarming frequency despite technologically advanced gloves and hand wraps. How much more danger is there when throwing an unprotected fist?

The Wing Chun vertical fist lands with the bottom three knuckles and the palm to the side. Old-school boxing, which was bare-knuckle you will recall, also did this – making western boxing and Wing Chun the world's only two vertical fist, straight hitting, counter attack methods of unarmed combat. But in recent times boxers have resorted to throwing their straight punches palm down. This isn't due to there being some new anatomical discovery or evidence that horizontal straight punches are superior to vertical straight punches. No. It's been due to the use of the boxing glove.

The boxing glove is rounded forward from the knuckles all the way to the fingertips and palm. This allows fighters to throw punches that nature frowns upon. This is also why so many "trained" fighters break their hands in street fights. The human skull is an unfriendly place to punch and if a man isn't careful and whacks his finger knuckles into a man's forehead, his hand is done. Mike Tyson was once in a fight at all all-night clothing store in Harlem back in the '80's with a fellow named Mitch "Blood" Green. We can forget about the foolishness of going shopping for clothes after midnight at establishments frequented by gentlemen with a nickname like Blood and focus on the fight itself. Tyson landed one of his vicious bent-arm blows – an overhand right against the much taller Green. The strike caused Green's eye to swell up like someone shoved a grapefruit under his eyelid but it also broke Tyson's hand. Some conflicting eyewitness testimony has it that despite Green's obvious injury, he was still ready to fight. Green, after all, could never have been confused with a male model in the first place so this facial disfiguration didn't depress or handicap him in the least. He was used to being ugly. Tyson, though, lost one of his two primary weapons and was in great pain. I'm not saying that he would have lost after this, but bodyguards and security apparently moved in to stop the fight at that point.

And the thing to remember about this incident is that it wasn't Mr. Green who injured Tyson. Tyson injured Tyson and he did this by executing his technique properly. It's not as though he failed to execute – he did. It's that the technique he performed – a horizontal bent-arm punch to the face – broke his hand. Let's not gloss over this because if we were to do this in a fight and not have bodyguards to bail us out, we may very well be seriously injured, perhaps killed, due to our error. All self-defenders should consider this carefully. Once again, it's not that Tyson didn't properly execute his technique under pressure and that error caused his injury. The problem wasn't one of performance but of improper method, which is to say a methodology that is in opposition to the facts of reality.

To think of this soberly, we see that the world's most dangerous fighter of that time – Tyson – was almost done in by his own weapon. Talk about a friendly fire accident! One wonders what would have happened had there been multiple assailants or no one to stop the fight. If you've ever trained with a gun instructor, you know that one of the big concerns before you ever pull a trigger is to make sure that you don't shoot someone (including yourself!) by accident. Any firearm coach worth his weight will preach endlessly about the basics: keep your finger off the trigger until you're ready to fire, don't point the weapon at anything you don't intend to shoot, always assume a gun is loaded until you do safety check, and – for crying out loud – make sure you know what's beyond your target. All firearm accidents – read that: someone getting shot that wasn't supposed to be – are the result of one of these errors, sometimes more.

I've heard it said that there are two types of gun owners: those that believe they might have a negligent discharge (accidental firing of the weapon) and those that have a negligent discharge. The point is that people who are overconfident and/or lazy violate the basics. It's the same thing with teaching the punch like this in the SLT form. Punching on instinct is fairly easy enough. Punching without breaking your hand or leaving yourself wide open is much harder. Such was the case with the former heavyweight champion of the world. He learned the hard way that punching without a boxing glove on is quite dangerous on the street.

This is precisely why Wing Chun favors the anatomically sound vertical fist punch. This isn't to say that you can't ever break your hand. Fighting is fighting and no matter how well trained you are, it's tough to control things. But your chances of hurting yourself – and thereby aid your enemy – is greatly reduced by punching in the correct and logical manner. But, remember, if you punch correctly, you won't hurt your hand. In Tyson's case his "correct" technique broke his hand. The horizontal fist is a creation of the modern gloved era. It's preferred within the ring or cage or anywhere men and women exchange blows with gloves on. But when we're discussing bare-knuckle combat, the vertical fist three-knuckle landing is the king.

The other great danger in swinging your punch is that it leaves you open. The great Jack Dempsey used to say that the more one opens their hook, the more they open their defense. Well, the same is certainly true of the straight punch. Defensively speaking, there is nothing worse than an aberrant offense, one that leads to you getting countered. It's akin to a quarterback throwing a pick-six interception except that in football at least the quarterback gets to come back on the field after the ensuing kickoff. In a fight, if you leave yourself open you could get knocked out.

Furthermore, there's also more danger in getting grabbed and taken down if your elbows aren't in to defend your trunk. Proper punching keeps your elbows and forearms inside so takedown defense is vastly improved.

Mistake #2 – Over-commitment

One of the other significant things that training SLT's straight punch will help you avoid is the mistake of over-extending your punch. By forcing the Wing Chun fighter into the uncomfortable YJKYM (at least when the student first starts) the system plants the seeds of proper muscle memory into the punch mechanism. At first, we're just throwing an arm punch. Using the hip and shoulder for added power and range (not to mention footwork) will come later in Chum Kiu.

But before the Wing Chun student can properly develop footwork and torque with their punching, they must learn to relax and let their punch snap to the target without going beyond the natural boundary of their reach. Throwing the straight punch thousands of times through the practice of the form gives the neuromuscular system ample opportunity to overcome the very human tendency to lean over at the waist in order to reach the target. Watch any novice hit a target and you'll see the tendency to lean over to gain distance. This is especially common when throwing the strong/power hand, which is for most people the right hand.

It simply isn't natural to throw a punch in a controlled fashion. The SLT straight punch sets the table for everything else that's going to come in the rest of the system by making sure we don't get knocked out first.

Overextending a punch causes three critical problems. First, it destroys one's balance momentarily and leaves the fighter with the task of recovering position instead of pressing the attack. Second, because the shoulders end up facing down, there is lag time before the next punch can be thrown because the other hand now has further to travel. Third, after throwing an overextended punch the puncher's face is generally closer to their foe, leaving them in peril of either being countered or grabbed. We often hear about many fights ending up on the ground. This is certainly overstated by grappling adherents but when it does happen it's often because one or both combatants overcommitted to their strikes and ended up falling into the hot zone.

Proper punch training, on focus mitts, hanging bags and so on, should commence immediately. The straight punch is the backbone of the system.

Mistake #3 – Dropping the hand

Connected to the problem of overextension is the dangerous habit of dropping your hand after punching, which leaves you exposed to being nailed with a good counter over the top. Proper and repeated practice of SLT will drill into you the habit of keeping the punching hand in line after the punch. This problem is so common that you can hardly spend five minutes in any fight gym without hearing someone say, "keep your hands up."

Mistake #4 – Stiffness

The other area that vex most people when it comes to straight hitting is that they are too stiff to make the punch work. They try and overcome this by simply swinging their blows at their foe but, of course, this has all sorts of other associated dangers that we'll get into later. Wing Chun remedies this by giving the student a chance to train slowly, loosely to develop good form.

The punch should not carry any tension until the very last second of the blow and then – and only then – there should be locking type whip as the fist fully tightens along with the wrist and arm. Hitting with a semi-closed fist not only endangers your hand but diminishes hitting power exponentially. It's like the difference between getting hit with a pillow or a bat. Both can be swung equally hard but obviously the softer object isn't going to cause considerable damage except, perhaps, make a fellow spill his drink. Immediately after this powerful tightening relaxation returns. In Wing Chun we refer to this as last second energy. Jack Dempsey, teaching the same concept in his description on straight hitting, called it a "convulsive grab." Either way, if you are stiff before or after the punch then you are losing both speed and power.

Carrying excess tension will cause a fighter to prematurely fatigue, telegraph, and have more difficulty making quick adjustments since change of direction will be difficult. It's like driving with your brakes on.

The Nine Advantages of Straight Hitting

A straight punch is always faster than a roundhouse punch.

A straight punch, as we've seen, is safer on your hand since your knuckles are aligned properly for impact and this lessens the chance of a fracture. They call it a "boxer's fracture" for a reason, after all.

A straight punch is less telegraphic. Even if you can't make yourself faster, you can make your enemy slower by giving him less time to react. Efficiency is the key. A telegraphed blow puts the puncher in jeopardy and lessens the impact of the blow should it land since the enemy saw it coming and may have begun moving away from it as a result.

Straight hitting preserves your balance better, which allows you to move freely while firing. This adds another level of speed for a fighter because they are able to literally hit and move at the same time – consistently. Roundhouse and/or angled blows do not allow you to do this. Only being able to hit from "the x" or the "top of the key" makes you, as far as application is concerned, slower in real fighting by allowing the enemy to be set to receive your attack. A mobile attacker, however, who is able to change angles while firing straight hits, puts the enemy in a tough spot since he has more decisions to make.

Straight hitting gives a fighter a higher rate of fire. You become fully automatic. The more compact and direct your blows, the faster they're going to be in combination. Overhand and roundhouse swings may be thrown fast but rarely, if ever, consecutively since they demand more balance and are less efficient. Many kids at our school are able to throw up to 10 full power punches in two seconds flat! Again – this isn't because these kids are especially gifted athletes. No. It's common because the mechanics of straight hitting allow for more combat efficiency than roundhouse blows.

Straight hitting is also more accurate than shots that have more air time. You're more likely to hit what you aimed at and this is kind of important. You simple can't miss fast enough. Accuracy of aim is critical.

Straight hitting keeps you a small target too. We have an old saying and I'm not sure where it came from: if your enemy can give a good description of you after the fight, you weren't hitting right. Literally, your face should be obscured by your blazing fast knuckles. Roundhouse shots open you up. Straight hits provide you offense and cover all at once.

Straight hitting, being more efficient, also requires less energy than roundhouse striking does. A serious consideration in taking a trip someplace is whether or not you have enough gas to get where you're going. Well, fighting is no different. It requires fuel and if a man runs out of endurance in a fight, he's toast. And don't listen to vacuous airheads that say things like "all fights are over in a few seconds anyway" as a way to disregard conditioning in a fight. No one knows how long any battle can last. Hopefully it's over in a few moments and you emerge victorious and with the admiration of men, the devotion of children, and the lust of women. But just in case it goes a little longer than expected, you don't want to be throwing around energy like there's no tomorrow. Straight hits, amidst all the previous advantages, are also most economical for your whole system. They preserve energy by requiring less movement.

Lastly, and perhaps least known and considered, is that straight hits are the most powerful blows one can throw. Yes, you read that right. A straight punch is more powerful than a roundhouse – if thrown properly. This requires a bit more elaboration than the rest.

First, most people are natural born brawlers - not punchers - and this must be trained out of them. Hence the punch this early in the Wing Chun form. Just because something is natural doesn't mean it's good. It's not a battle between processed foods and fruit, for goodness sake. A swing is the hallmark of an untrained fighter. The fact that many score blows that drop a man with such swings is due to the fact that swings of this nature often land on the foe's chin – the knockout button. This gives the impression of great power. But's it's a false impression.

This isn't to say that a puncher can't get some power from a swing – obviously they can. But the more the arm is straightened in a swing, and the less the elbow propels the strike (as an engine of the hip and shoulder) the weaker the blow. The power of any blow is dependent upon both the speed and the body mass of the strike. Remember that bit about mass times acceleration from school or were you too busy looking at girls? Either way, it's the same thing. In Wing Chun we call this structure; Dempsey referred to it as the power-line. The hip, shoulder, elbow, all the way through to the pinky knuckle – that's the proper alignment of a good punch.

This is why a straight hit is so powerful. It maximizes the use of body mass. A swing is a dead arm blow – just the weight of the arm and that's all (though that might still hurt, of course).

Question: how much can you bench press compared to dumbbell fly? See? And how much can you squat or leg press compared to leg abduction?

Properly learned straight hitting is the most powerful means of striking available to the human body. This is why it's the foundation of Wing Chun striking. We may use angle blows as needed. But straight hitting, for all the aforementioned reasons, form the logical foundation of Wing Chun combat striking.

Kicking

Though it isn't shown directly, the jik tek – or straight kick – is implied in the punch section of the SLT form. As we've covered, nearly every mistake in Wing Chun application is a mistake of one or more of the first four sections of SLT. The neglect of proper kicking is probably a close second to the neglect of logical footwork in the pantheon of Wing Chun errors. This happens often because, for one, the kick is merely implied in the first form, and, secondly, the hand techniques are far more unique and, therefore, cool, so the Wing Chun fighter ignores his legs as a primary means of attack and defense.

Truly, this is a mistake. It's like an NFL team only using the running game and refusing to pass because they identify as a running team.

Like with the punch, the Wing Chun straight kick should be thrown without wind-up or telegraph. Imagine if your hands were hanging loosely at your sides and you went to throw a punch. You'd still throw the punch as straight as possible, vertical fist style, and the focus of the impact would be with the bottom three knuckles. Well, it's pretty much the same thing with the kick too. The straight kick is launched like an exaggerated step. It uses no wind-up and, like the punch, it should be thrown with snapping power as the weapon whips up from the floor. Also, the heel is used to strike whenever possible. Because the kick is used quite often below the waist, the heel can sometimes not land directly so using the ball or flat of the foot is acceptable as well. The idea is to use the bottom of the foot much like you would use the bottom knuckles in a punch.

The straight kick and straight punch are the twin terrors of Wing Chun. Their potency is lost on many people because they appear so simple. Don't make that mistake. Master them both.

The application of kicks is and must be integrated into the rest of the core Wing Chun concepts. The use of footwork to create angles and distance will maximize the efficacy of your kicks – and your kicks, used smartly, will increase the potency of your punches. All of this, of course, will heighten your in-fighting skill by giving you overall command of the engagement. We must always remember that these principles of combat are interrelated to one another. The use of footwork – angles, side steps and pivots – in order to nullify the enemy's attack through position and timing will increase your ability to land heavy counter-attacks. To the uneducated, it will appear that you're simply firing willy-nilly and somehow your hits are getting through while your enemy's strikes are not. But it's the other principles that allow for this and it's the epitome of simultaneous attack and defense.

Although the heel is usually the part of the foot we strike with on the basic kick, the ball of the foot can be used as well. Either way, like with the punch, aim with the bottom of the foot. Practice this kick thousands of times to master it.

The straight kick plays a huge role in the actualization of this goal. At the moment of violence, the Wing Chun fighter will, if possible, close the gap before the enemy has a chance to get mobilized. But closing the gap requires footwork. As we saw with the punch, if the target is past the distance the punch can be safely executed, we should not just go busting forward. This causes us to get overextended and makes us tremendously vulnerable to counter-attack. A kick, therefore, should almost always precede a punch or any hand technique in such encounters. The kick literally paves the way for the follow up inside (close-range) assault. Generally, this straight kick is thrown to the enemy's legs or waist area. Thrown properly, without telegraph, it's extraordinarily difficult to see coming, making defense against it quite precarious. Furthermore, because it can land literally anywhere on the body – from head to toe (kicking high is, of course, fine if you can) - it's even more vexing for the bad guy. Couple that with the increased power a kick has over a punch and you can see why you should seek to kick at every opportunity.

In the event that the enemy has mobilized his attack before you were able to cut him off (stop hit), a fast side-step followed by a blistering low line kick works superbly. The idea is that the Wing Chun system is set up so that footwork and striking – using hand and leg attacks – can happen most expeditiously. The enemy should get no rest – nor a good chance to face you directly. He should be having to turn while at the same time defend against low line and high line attacks. Many Wing Chun fighters fail to use footwork based on the chui-ying/by-ying principle, march straight forward to get inside and rely almost exclusively on hand techniques. This makes them vastly easier to counter-attack and, again, underscores the misunderstanding of the system's core principles put forth in the opening of the SLT form.

In this way, you can begin to see how Wing Chun achieves the proper balance of aggressiveness without being reckless. This is no small distinction.

Remember: once the fight has started (for whatever reason), start moving to both deny your enemy a target and to launch your own offensive. The footwork, basic kick, and basic punch are initially taught separately but the goal is to use them as one rapid and destructive integrated whole. The beauty of the system is that integration is always assumed at every point. For example, imagine that you begin the *cho-ma* sidestep as your enemy launches a haymaker. As your right foot carries you out of the way, you turn your trunk and instead of bringing your left foot fully with you, you throw a hard, snappy straight kick with it instead. Then you follow up with a burst of punches, followed by yet another hard kick.

You're starting to get the idea.

Wing Chun & Muay Thai

Another point to note, you can't do such things when you use roundhouse style weaponry. Roundhouse strikes – especially with kicks – will open up your centerline, break your balance, strike with parts of your body that are easy to hurt (top of your foot, ankle, instep compared to the bottom of your foot) and lengthen your recovery time.

It's generally assumed that Muay Thai is a better kicking method than Wing Chun. In the main, this is true but it's true not due to the merits of the respective systems but because of the illogical and unwarranted rejection of Wing Chun's core principles. We repeat: that Muay Thai is a better kicking art presently than Wing Chun is due to the Wing Chun student's erroneous understanding of the core principles. The moment this is corrected, proper training in the system should commence and the student will (through hours of practice) gain the full use of the arsenal Wing Chun puts at his/her disposal.

Muay Thai focuses immensely upon its formidable kicking arsenal, which is much to its credit. The thing is, it's renowned for its pulverizing round-kick whereas it's the push-kick that's the best kick in their toolbox. The push-kick, if you don't know, is basically Muay Thai's version of the Wing Chun straight kick. The reason the push-kick of Muay Thai isn't used more is because it makes for more defensive matches due to the superiority of straight hits over roundhouse strikes. But a defensive match is bad entertainment for all the gamblers and ruffians who prefer blood and mayhem to skill and defense. Boring matches are a hard sell. So, in all, follow the money. The straight kick is, like the straight punch or jab, the preeminent tool in all of fighting, regardless of style. It's not for lack of effectiveness that it isn't more popular – in fact, it's precisely because of its efficacy that it doesn't get more use. When I was learning Muay Thai as a young man, my coach said that a fighter with a great push-kick could hardly be touched. He said that for self-defense, especially when you have shoes on, this simple kick was better and safer to use than the round-kick.

In all, though, please don't consider this as an attack on Muay Thai. In fact, it should be evident that Wing Chun is much more similar to it than most of us think. The errors at issue are ones of poor training and tactical philosophy.

17

CONTACT & INFIGHTING

We now arrive at the fourth part of the SLT form. At this point we're introduced to two very important "seed" hands. They're called seed hands precisely because they each have multiple application possibilities. They are the *tan-sao* and then the *fook-sao*. We pause to consider that this is the slowest section of the form – the slowest of any part of any form or drill in Wing Chun really – and this is done to reinforce critical information.

First, we must understand that this section is concerned with the contact phase or clinch part of the fight. Most people think of clinching and they think of boxers in a tie-up, grapplers looking to wrestle their man down to the mat, or Muay Thai fighters using the neck hold to deliver knees and elbows. The thing is, though, the Wing Chun fighter is, as we've already covered, not interested in winning a sport match. The inside game is the most dangerous place one can be in a fight by virtue of the fact that all of the body's vulnerable targets are easily accessed. Also, one's balance might easily be destroyed at this range too. This being the case, Wing Chun takes a highly nuanced (though simple) view of the fight at this range and it's here that the system is perhaps most unique.

When in close, Wing Chun seeks to control the arms/hands or the enemy. This is a critical aspect of its combat realism. Nearly every other fighting method seeks to control the body of the enemy, thereby leaving their hands free. This can easily lead to a weapon being pulled.

The first order of business is to keep yourself as safe as possible. When there is no contact with the enemy this is achieved through the use of footwork and straight hitting. Once on the inside, though, it's achieved through the disruption and control of the enemy's balance. This is exactly what good MMA and grappling fighters do on the inside as well. They tie up their opponent and try and control their balance. If you've ever had the chance to clinch with both a boxer and a wrestler you'll notice immediately that the latter is much stronger than the former and attempts to throw you around. In boxing, this is illegal, of course, so there's no need to develop this skill. But the point is that the Wing Chun fighter is also looking to control their enemy's balance at this range. The difference is that in Wing Chun the fighter is also attempting to both attack and defend the soft targets of the eyes, jaw, throat, neck and groin.

This is a critical distinction because sport-based systems offer no defense against scientific attacks to these areas. They're illegal, after all (and absolutely should be in all combat sports!) so there's no need to develop defenses for them.

But a strike to the eyes followed by a shot to the wind pipe is serious business. Let's take a look at how Wing Chun approaches the issue. To my knowledge, there is no other empty hand fighting system on the planet that systematically covers this range as logically as Wing Chun.

Proper inside control doesn't just open up strikes to the high-line, but kicks as well. Some of Wing Chun's most dangerous tools are its close-range kicks that can cripple a foe while still controlling their hands.

Purpose of Tan & Fook Sao
And What Ali can teach us about Wing Chun

We need to be clear on something about Wing Chun. It's unique and, for those of us that like it, it's fantastically cool. No other system uses hand techniques quite the same way. There's a smoothness to the movements and, when doing drills with a partner where you're tying them up and hitting them at the same time, there's an almost euphoric sense of both sophistication and power. There's nothing else like it. If you've been training in this system for any length of time you know what I mean.

This, however, is exactly the danger.

The very fact that the inside techniques are so cool are precisely what makes them dangerous to us as practitioners. In short, when the *sao* becomes the focus rather than our enemy, we have a serious problem. A quick glance at Wing Chun forums and Facebook groups will prove unequivocally that many students of the method obsess over the nuances of technique while not giving much thought to how to apply the technique.

We must train ourselves to think of every technique we meet in the forms as *a structural foundation of an application limited only by our need and/or imagination*. This is the mantra of my Sifu, Tony Massengill. He also likes to remind his students to never look at a technique and ask, "what is it?" but, rather, "what can it do?"

As always, a good way to make a mess of things is to argue from the unknown to the known. It's always a good idea to keep the reverse in order – which is to say, reason from things we know to be true and have seen, to the things we haven't seen and aren't sure of (the unknown). In this case boxing can be very helpful because when we look at it we see a great diversity of application style despite its apparent lack of technique[1].

Muhammad Ali was a rather peculiar boxer. Since he's been retired for so long it's easy to dismiss how spectacularly eccentric his approach was at the time. He carried his hands dangerously low. He bounced around on his toes. He leaned backwards against punches. He never went to the body and rarely ever ducked. Also, he didn't try to hit very hard – preferring speed and volume over power – and he had the temerity to actually talk to his opponent while boxing.

If any boxing coach in the world taught a novice to do these things they'd be guilty of malpractice as these habits are violations of a great many fundamentals of the game. But, alas! These "mistakes" were the hallmark of not just a good boxer, but arguably the greatest of all time (which, of course, the ever-humble Ali had no trouble telling people).

He made up for these stylistic peculiarities with a unique mix of attributes and strategy.

You see, Ali was a heavyweight and heavyweights are not usually the most mobile group of fighters. By developing a style that was heavy on movement (and early in his career, Ali was a veritable motion machine) he exploited a great weakness in everyone else's game: lack of footwork. His opponents simply weren't ready to deal with such a mobile target. They were trained to fight a certain way and that was it. Ali's movement and refusal to fight on the inside proved to be an insurmountable challenge while he was in his prime. Opponents couldn't catch him. It was that simple.

He coupled this with fantastic speed and timing. A slower fighter never would have been able to make this style work. Another overlooked aspect of Ali – perhaps because of the way he fought (like a little guy) – was that he was actually a fairly big heavyweight for his day. With only a few exceptions – George Foreman being one, and even that being a slight difference – Ali was usually the bigger man in the ring. This made his hit-and-move tactics that much more effective. He didn't need to go to the body because he was tall enough, and fast enough, to stay on the outside. And he could pull straight back from punches because he was moving. An immobile fighter leaning backwards is asking for serious trouble, but no one could catch up to the fleet footed heavyweight.

Lastly, and we saw this (sadly) late in his career when some of those great reflexes had begun to fade, that he possessed a nearly indestructible chin. So, when his opponents finally did catch him and detonate bombs (think Frazier, Foreman and Shavers, some of the greatest hitters in boxing history), Ali was able to take their best shots.

What does this have to do with Wing Chun? Well, despite how bizarre Ali's tactics sometimes were, he was obviously quite effective. There were many – especially early in his career – that criticized his style and said there was no way it would work. They were adamant. The great Cus D'Amato, trainer of Mike Tyson, was an early and vocal critic. He complained that Ali's bouncing robbed him of power and that he'd never be able to deal with a stronger puncher that could take his space away. Do you see where we're going with this? Everyone has presuppositions about what's real or not, and what will work in reality. But the final arbiter is always reality. In the end, Ali proved even to his detractors that he was the real deal despite his stylistic creativity. This humbled an entire generation of boxing coaches and it should inform us as well.

Also worthy of our consideration is that once Ali came back from his exile (due to his refusal to be inducted into the Armed Services during the Vietnam War) he wasn't quite the same fighter. He'd clearly lost a little speed during the three-year layoff[2]. To compensate for this, he used the clinch quite a bit more than he had when he was faster. The point to understand is that the goal of self-defense is always good defense. If you don't have good defense, there's no way to stop your enemy. There are two ways to control the attacker so as to stymie his offense: distance control and evasion or the clinch. Ali's career is a great example of both of these in action. In his prime years, no one could reach him; later, the slower version used the clinch to smother attacks when he could.

Thus, Wing Chun specializes in clinch-fighting. The *tan-sao and fook-sao*, therefore, represent the two types of clinch positions your hands will be in (preferably) for professional in-fighting.

Contact & Infighting | 151

You see, tan sao and fook sao are contact (clinching) range tools used to achieve the needed integration of offense and defense on the inside. The tan represents any contact hand position that's inside your enemy's hand. The fook represents any covering hand or top hand position. Accordingly, the tan action "spreads" toward the enemy's shoulder because if your inside hand sits on the centerline you will expose your flank (or outer gate) to quick attack. Likewise, the fook "rides" the center. It flows toward the enemy's middle, or center-mass, because if the covering hand is flowing toward the shoulder (on the near side) it will expose your middle.

This is the key to understanding the Wing Chun inside game.

Really. It's that simple.

But I said simple, not easy.

The point to remember is that if you're in range to hit the eye, throat and jaw, so is he. The goal isn't simply to hit those targets, it's to use structure and position to nullify his attack (keeping yourself as safe as possible) and then taking advantage of his mistakes (under-corrections and over-corrections) to launch your safe attack. To trade strikes at this range is extraordinarily dangerous. The goal is control. As Sifu Tony Massengill reminds me all the time: "if I can hit you, maybe you can hit me...but if I can control you, I can hit you without getting hit back." This is a fighting mantra he learned directly from Ip Ching, Ip Man's son.

That's our goal with this section of the form. It's the introduction of the contact/inside game of fighting from the Wing Chun perspective where the tan sao and fook sao actions take precedence because it's exactly these "shapes" and structures that allow us to fulfill the goal of striking while controlling the enemy.

Many people miss this all-important tactical goal and focus too much on the precision of the technique. This achieves the end of making the Wing Chun fighter a tremendous drill fighter rather than a real fighter. This is what you see on some of those crazy Wing Chun forums where people endlessly criticize without reference to application. They're like those guys that railed against Ali for having his hands down because they were blind to the fact that he didn't need his hands up because his footwork rendered his enemy's attack futile.

Ali kept the main thing the main thing. If you can't hit me, you can't beat me. Others, forgetting the main goal, being devoid of logical foundation theory, saw only the fact that his hands were down, and railed against him. But you have your hands up when you're in range in order to keep yourself safe. What if you aren't in range, though? What if you use footwork and angles to keep your opponent from getting at you?

This is the point to keep in mind about Wing Chun. When you're on the outside (or free movement range, if you prefer), you "control" your enemy by means of lightning footwork (don't let him face you... and if he can, don't let him reach you...and if he can, clinch with him). When on the inside, you need contact control. If you don't have some type of control over him you're in great danger. I repeat: if you are on the inside and don't have accountability of his bridge (controlling his balance and/or offense) then you likely shouldn't launch an attack until you do. You may, indeed, get away with firing willy-nilly now and then. But this is like driving through an intersection with your eyes closed (which is what driver's in my city do apparently, but that's another story). You might get away with it...until you don't. It's not a good idea.

A quick way to see the integration of all this is with the following example.

Let's say that a bad guy steps forward and launches an overhand right punch at you. How should we respond? Well, what do the core principles of the SLT form teach us? Let's remember that the bad guy is not throwing a "demo" punch. This is the real thing, in all its sound and fury. He isn't going to pull the punch. Moreover, he isn't likely to stop there and leave his arm hanging in the air either. After the punch, he's most likely to throw another punch, or duck and try and tackle you, or he'll move back out of the way. We repeat: he won't just stand there and see what you're going to do. Real fights are not demos.

Well, standing still and trying to block the strike is literally the last thing we want to do for the simple reason that the bad guy has the initiative. He's ahead of us in the action/reaction cycle (sometimes referred to as the OODA loop...which we'll explain in another volume). We'd prefer to stop-hit him with a straight kick or punch but if he's got the jump on us, the SLT principle of facing/not-facing suggests that we should move in order to take away his positional advantage.

That being the case, let's say that we side-step (cho ma) to our right – moving us off the line of our incoming opponent. This serves three purposes. First, it makes the punch miss. Second, it nullifies any follow-up he may have intended (which is why using footwork for defense is generally preferable to blocking). And thirdly, it facilitates a facing/not-facing position to our favor. Now the enemy has to turn to us with a follow-up. If he does, let's say that we cut him off by stepping in (we had the angle, remember?) with a pak sao (a type of fook sao) that takes both his balance and left arm out of play. At the same time, we punch.

If he were to shoot backwards or sideways to get out of the way, we could pursue with a battering array of low-line kicks as we push and yank him.

This is just one example of how in very short order we have an amazing interplay of the core concepts from the first four sections of the SLT form. It was simple, yes, but not easy. An attack was launched. We use footwork based off the YJKYM, gain an angle from the facing principle using that footwork, and then take control of his balance and shut his offense down with the *fook sao* principle while simultaneously hitting him with the straight punch.

At every turn we must avoid the mistake of focusing on one principle at the exclusion of the others. The key is integration as no one principle can stand on its own.

For example, the facing principle always, always, always implies control of position. If you have no accountability for the bad guy's offense, then other principles might not come into play because you could get knocked out before applying them. The *jeet* principle – the stop-hit – is a masterful stroke but it's a resounding mistake to stay in the line of fire in the event you didn't have the timing and/or accuracy at that precise moment to stop the enemy.

Also, the forward pressure principle (which we'll get to in a little bit) is often abused mindlessly without reference to the other core principles like proper bridging (gaining the clinch), facing, etc. If we play one core principle over against the others, we're making a critical error.

The *fook sao* is done three times in SLT with exacting slowness. This has several purposes – both technical (like developing the proper mechanics of moving the elbow to the centerline via the elbow-moving-line) and tactical. The tactical principle most associated with the *fook sao* action is called *lat sau jik chung*. The translation of this into English is a bit clunky but it means, for the most part, that the Wing Chun fighter should be seeking to flow towards openings at the centerline. Some say, "lost hand thrust forward."

This is all fine and good except that not all other fighting styles are concerned with protecting their centerline. A modern MMA fighter often leaves his middle open in order to entice you to take a shot at his center so that he can duck to throw an overhand. A blind adherence to the *lat sau jik chung* principle, therefore, could prove to be the downfall of the overzealous Wing Chun fighter. But only if he has first neglected the facing/not-facing principle and/or the control principle of the tan and *fook* hands. (Incidentally, this is all quite hard to convey in written form which is exactly why we have video instruction on this and similar points).

More on the Fook Sao

It's been said that the *fook sao* isn't really a technique per se but is a structure that's the building block for specific applications. One way to see this is that the *fook sao*, with the hand cupped in during the form, is developing two details of critical importance – one technical and the other technical/tactical.

First, by leaving the hand in that position, the practitioner is focusing on the elbow moving the arm and hand. Left to our own devices, students always tend to focus on the hand rather than the elbow. This causes a loss of power through bad mechanics since the hand isn't driven by the structure anymore. As it goes, the elbow connects to the structure, which is to say to the floor. The slow *fook sao* practice in SLT is designed to teach the Wing Chun student the proper, non-contradictory basis for power delivery on the inside.

If Wing Chun doesn't make us more efficient, better protected, more powerful and quicker than the enemy on the inside (where things can go wrong in a furious hurry), then it's useless. The crude core of any fighting art/science must be this: to be able to damage the enemy while not letting the enemy damage you. To achieve this critical balance Wing Chun teaches us the *fook sao*.

This seems weird, I know. But the stance is spring loaded; you're a coiled spring. And you're training with the *fook sao* in order to develop power through the YJKYM. I can't emphasize this enough. Proper power generation is essential because without it the student will either be easily overpowered on the inside, or they'll resort to shoulder torque or static force generation (through stiffness).

Many Wing Chun students don't have real power in their technique. Watch Muay Thai fighters, as well as MMA and boxing students, and compare them to the average Wing Chun fighter. What usually jumps out at me (besides the lack of aliveness in most Wing Chun footwork) is a dangerous power deficit. Wing Chun students, because of poor instruction, think that being "soft" will overcome power. No, it won't. Not the way they define softness. We define softness as relaxed power, which is achieved through good form/structure. The point to keep front and center is that good form/structure is loading us to deliver maximum payload without compromising our stance. The *fook sao* practice connects the pieces, so to speak and trains us to use coiled-spring type energy based on strong mechanics of the YJKYM.

Power generation for all-out fighting is a careful business because one has to worry about getting pushed, pulled, and tackled as well as hit. MMA fighters throw their punches (especially on the inside) different than boxers for this reason. If they over-torque a hook, they leave themselves wide open for a takedown. Wing Chun at its heart is an anti-grappling system, so its striking is always from a stable core that radiates stored energy. (Incidentally, some instructors teach their students to lean back in their YJKYM like they're facing a hurricane force wind. This is nonsense. The goal of the stance is to make you a mobile coiled spring).

On the other factor – stiffness – many people confuse the early lessons of relaxation with being told not to use power. In reality, we want to use as much power as possible. The issue is that most novices will try and generate power through wild, unfocused stiffness. They push everything. But this compromises their structure and obliterates their ability to adapt to changes. To be soft is to be explosive! The idea is to be able to use "last second energy" and this requires relaxation. Stiffness will give you strength but not true power because fighting power is and must be explosive. And doing the *fook sao* so slowly – and three times in a row – helps root out the "deal with the devil" that stiffness is.

The second technical detail involved here is the aforementioned concept of *lat sau jik chung*. The natural tendency for students is to "chase hands." This is to say that if there's an incoming strike, the default setting of a novice is to use a block that follows the enemy's limb past the centerline. In Wing Chun, however, the goal is to be as direct and efficient as possible, so we see this as wasted movement. I ask my students all the time, "...would you rather have me grab your arm really hard or hit you in the throat?" Obviously, you aren't going to win a fight with a *pak sao*.

So, the *fook sao* practice here in SLT is designed to help the student overcome the natural tendency to follow, or baby-sit, an incoming limb. Instead, we want "chase the center, not the hand." Like we said before, though, this principle, as integral as it is to success, has to be applied wisely – especially when dealing with grapplers and MMA fighters of our modern era. The principle still applies, please note, it just needs to be adapted (as all theory has to be applied in practice) to the circumstances. We never want to baby-sit the enemy's arm when we could be hitting him and/or taking his balance away – with the noted exception of there being a weapon in his hand!

These two principles of proper power generation and chasing and controlling the center are quite unique to the Wing Chun system. Also, when combined with the proper understanding of bridge control already referenced, you can see why this part of the SLT form is so important.

18

IDOLATRY IN WING CHUN

THE CASE AGAINST TRADITIONALISM

Let's begin by defining what we mean by the term *traditionalism*. It means the unwavering commitment to preserving a past approach. A traditional approach to Wing Chun, therefore, means practicing and applying the method in the precise manner it was passed down from previous teachers and ancestors. In this event, the focus of the training – that is, its primary goal – is not application, but preservation of previous practice. Of course, the traditionalist will object to this characterization. They will say they are focused on application by way of their adherence to the past. Nevertheless, it can't be claimed that there is a higher objective than the preservation of the method due to the internal pressures of the lineage.

It would seem that Wing Chun is, for the most part, full of its share of schools where deviation from the past is frowned upon. In such schools it's quite evident that the core of the training philosophy is not individuation of the material but conformity. This is because of the philosophy of traditionalism.

It's our contention that traditionalism is illogical on several fronts and should be summarily rejected by everyone who desires to learn self-defense. Furthermore, the philosophy of traditionalism is not just illogical but dangerous too – primarily because we're talking about a fighting method, not a dance style. It's also our contention that traditionalism is utterly destroying Wing Chun for the simple reason that it places the emphasis of training on maintaining a thing (the traditional method) rather than on applying that thing.

A few years ago, my son, who is a great fan of baseball and its robust history, took part in a throwback game between the Shoeless Joe Jackson museum and the Ty Cobb museum. The game was played according to the old dead-ball rules and was replete with replica uniforms and the whole shebang. Everyone had a delightful time full of laughter and camaraderie as well as awe over how different the game was 100 years ago. Not only that, but a few vendors showed up too. One was a food truck from which I ordered possibly the greatest hot dog any man has ever had in the history of frankfurters. Really. I had no idea a hot dog could be that good.

Anyway...

It was all quite an innocent and charming way to share with a new generation the history of the game as well as teach about the excellencies of the aforementioned great players. This was especially true of Shoeless Joe who is, incidentally, banned from the Hall of Fame in Cooperstown due to the Black Sox scandal surrounding the 1919 World Series (*"say it ain't so, Joe"*). As you can imagine, it wasn't a very well attended event as not many people care to come out for an afternoon of nostalgia except for serious baseball history-buffs. Anyway, there's nothing at all the matter with a bunch of people doing such a thing. It's all fun.

Likewise, I enjoy historical battlefields as well. Just a few weeks ago I brought the family to Chattanooga, Tennessee where we visited the Lookout Mountain battlefield and I marveled over the whole place – especially the troop movements over such difficult terrain. Imagine having to climb a mountain just to get shot at, for goodness sake. That's probably only exceeded in unpleasantness by a trip to your in-laws for Christmas. Anyway, I've gone to others, like Cowpens which was the site of Tarleton's stunning defeat in the *Revolutionary War*, and witnessed men and women re-enacting the event. This all serves a great purpose for society – to remember our collective past.

But if the U.S. military suddenly started to arm its soldiers with muskets again, we would all agree they had lost their minds. Surely the principles of war are the same – to kill the enemy and break his stuff - but the means through which we do that in the modern era has changed vastly. Indeed, at West Point they still study Sun Tzu's classic. Those principles are timeless. It's the application of those principles that has changed. This is what our argument is for Wing Chun. The principles ought to be passed down; they're timeless. But the particulars – things like the drills and application tactics – must be jettisoned the moment they get in the way of progress.

This is to say that we can and should honor our past. Personally, I love history – which you probably gathered from my choice of vacations and leisure. But we must be on-guard against using the past as a means of refusing to adapt to the present. True, the balance of these things is an arduous task and no man or group can claim they get the balance perfect. Nevertheless, we stave off disaster by avoiding the extremes of neglecting history outright and/or worship of the past.

And this brings us to the chief reason for the resounding error of traditionalism in Wing Chun: the elevation of the method to the point where it operates as a de facto religion.

You see, we can and should study the warriors of the past – especially their tactics. But we shouldn't idolize them. That's utter foolishness and, quite frankly, open idolatry. Nathaniel Greene's brilliant use of the terrain and his enemy's aggressiveness, not to mention Tarleton's high contempt for colonial militia, teaches us great lessons about knowing our enemy and fighting to our strengths. Boxing does the same thing. Watching Ali outwit George Foreman in the famous Zaire *rope-a-dope* fight is exhilarating and proves how right Sun Tzu was about the art of deception and accurately knowing one's enemy (since Ali used Foreman's aggression and lack of discipline to tire him out).

The error is when Eastern ancestor worship meets and mingles with idolatry of a fighting method – in this case, Wing Chun. There's a great difference between studying the tactics of the past and being bound by them.

The issue at hand, to be clear, is idolatry and idolatry is anything or person that becomes an end in and of itself except for God. God alone is an end in Himself. If something else can claim that distinction then that person or thing must, quite naturally, be the ultimate thing in the universe. Everything else in the universe, save for God, has a limited being and/or function and to make these limited (or derivative) things ultimate in one's mind is to turn them into that which they're not. This leads to a distortion of their function, destroying both the subject and object involved in the idolatry.

To the western ear, the notion of idolatry strikes us as a rather odd, even archaic business. We think, with some condescension frankly, that no one does that anymore by virtue of the fact that we don't see people bowing down to statues. But that's a rather torpid definition of the term. It's best to see it in terms of one's basic heart-commitment. The question of *ultimacy* is the thing. What is ultimate? In the case of Wing Chun, since it can't be an ultimate thing (it's a creation of man, after all), the big idea is using Wing Chun for the purpose of self-defense. That's the context and the great Wong Shun Leung was correct when he said that one shouldn't be Wing Chun's slave but should make it ours. That's the proper context. Wing Chun's purpose is to serve – to be used. A switch in philosophical focus to having one serve *it* makes Wing Chun one's idol. No created thing can be an end in and of itself. That's philosophically impossible. In that way, the questions always beg: where from and what for?

This might all sound a bit too theological for the discussion but that doesn't make it untrue. Idolatry is, in another way of saying it, the act of ascribing God's attributes and qualities to created things. It is, be sure, the supreme violation of reality and the root of mankind's greatest travails. We see that so much in the subject of economics when people make the acquisition of money and things the highest good. The Bible speaks of the love of money being the source of all kinds of crap in society (literally using the Greek word *kakos*). People often misconstrue the gist of this statement, though. The Bible nowhere states that wealth (and the productivity that yields wealth) is a bad thing. It's the idolatry of money that leads to evil. Idolatry ruins everything it touches because it's a violation of God's natural order of life. Making money is fine; worshipping money is the problem.

We know that traditionalism is a result of such idolatry when we hear people speak of "pure" Wing Chun. And when you hear people speak of such things it invariably follows that the goal of the training is Wing Chun itself rather than the actual function of a fighting system – that is, to aid human beings in the moral endeavor of self-defense. Thus, the means supplant the actual goal for which they are intended to serve. Idolatry is always a foundational distortion of reality. After all, for a person to defend themselves from an aggressor is a morally right thing to do and God has wired His creation so that men of discipline, skill, wisdom and courage are always in the advantage over against those that are barbaric savages. Wing Chun, in this way, is a glorious moral achievement. It's a logical and objectively true means of overcoming the greatest evil on earth possible between human beings: the initiation of force. If, though, Wing Chun becomes the goal itself, rather than a means to an end, it becomes a context within itself and, consequently, ends up losing its function.

All things under the sun have a purpose, a function, and cannot be seen as an end in and of themselves. There's an old saying that I've seen in a meme, which goes something like, "people are supposed to be loved and things used...our problem is that we love things and use people." Quite frankly, that's true but it's true precisely because man has an idolatry problem, which deforms and twists life from its actual purpose to one of false religion.

So, this is the foundational error impacting the whole debate. Idolatry leads to the fallacious presumption that somewhere there exists in reality an unstained ideal in Wing Chun – an exemplary approach, nearly divine in its origin. The error in this thinking ought to be rather evident to one and all – inviting the skepticism and scorn any would have to a street-corner vendor selling a tonic purported to roll back the ravages of age. Simply put, there is no *pure* Wing Chun. There never was and there never could be because for there to be a pure Wing Chun requires there to be a pure person that created it, right? Are we really saying such nonsense as this?

Furthermore, it's a logical necessity that for there to be a pure Wing Chun, which is to say a perfect Wing Chun, there must have been a personal embodiment of that approach. After all, Wing Chun, or any fighting art for that matter, isn't a metaphysical-given; it isn't a fact of nature. On the contrary, it's a man-created system intended to assist human beings in the task of keeping themselves as safe as possible in the event of a violent encounter (the logical definition of self-defense among civilians). Wing Chun, not being the ocean, the mountains, or some pristine meadow, exists only because men and women have applied themselves to the task and study of self-defense. Thus, for there to be a pure Wing Chun – read that: perfect – there would have to have been a pure and perfect person to create it.

This also leads to another problem. Even if there was a "pure" Wing Chun, how is the student to attain that level of perfection? If Ip Man was pure, how is it that his students could claim the same quality? And what exactly is that quality? See where this is going? The proper view of Wing Chun as a tool to be used by individuals for the purpose of improving their self-defense skills avoids all this folly. If Jimi Hendrix taught you to play guitar that's pretty cool. You'd have a story to tell everyone indeed. But it wouldn't matter that you couldn't play like Jimi. That's not the point. The goal would be to play the guitar. If the goal was to be Jimi Hendrix, no one could do that except Jimi Hendrix.

In this way, music doesn't suffer from the idolatry of traditionalism like martial arts does. We can be a fan of Hendrix *and* a guitar player, but one isn't necessary for the other. All Hendrix fans aren't guitar players and not all guitar players have to be fans of Hendrix. Literature is the same way. I'm a huge fan of both Hemingway and Hugo and those men had vastly different styles. I'm also writing this. If the point of studying literature was to copy the past, I wouldn't be writing this. I'd be busy transcribing *For Whom the Bell Tolls* or writing commentary on it.

In short, neither Hendrix, nor Hugo, nor Ip Man or anyone/anything else in all creation is God. *Purple Haze, Old Man and the Sea, Ninety-Three and Sil Lim Tao* are not the Word of the Lord. Learning to play guitar or write doesn't mean that we worship the heroes of the past – adore them, yes; worship them, no. But this is exactly the sort of nonsensical foolishness we're left with when we get into such debates over Wing Chun. Traditional Wing Chun, that is, doing it exactly as your ancestors did it, is plainly idolatrous and turns a useful system of self-defense into a religion.

Ah, the insanity of it all! Again, we ask, was *Ip Man* or *Ng Mui* or *Wong Shun Leung* perfect? Were they, in fact, pure? If not, then what divine spark elevated them in such a way that they transcended their human flaws, the limitations of their faculties of reason, and presented them with the golden-scrolls of pure Wing Chun? This isn't meant in any way to attack those titans of fistic history. Instead, it's meant to shine a needed ray of light upon the dark corner of the preposterous notion of any martial art being beyond human hands and elevated into the realm of Godliness.

We should like to apologize for having to drag the reader through a discourse on theology in our rebuttal of Wing Chun traditionalism, but the plain fact of the matter is that it has to be done. Furthermore, once we see this root issue and discern for ourselves how it plays out, how it ruins everything it touches, we can correct the error. To omit it for the reason that not all readers are Christian or religious is to leave open the door for the error to creep in again[1]. If we merely say that traditionalism is impractical and don't dismantle its root error, that being theological/philosophical, it will assuredly come again. So, the root of the error lies in its idolatry, which is to say in the elevation of a derivative thing (Wing Chun) to the position of ultimate thing. This obliterates the proper goal of Wing Chun, which is applied self-defense. Understanding this error will protect both us and the system we love by keeping all in their proper context.

Insofar as we achieve this proper balance, thereby returning Wing Chun to its rightful place as merely a means to an end, we protect the art from sure ruination and eventual extinction. It's patently obvious that methods like MMA and boxing are advanced in the realm of hand-to-hand sport-fighting. All but the most delusional soul admits that skilled practitioners of these disciplines are formidable fighters. It's also obvious that these disciplines, though honoring their past by studying their heroes, are not bound by them. In this way, both boxing and MMA are free from the religious impulses that Wing Chun (and martial arts in general) often falls prey to.

Boxing and MMA have their pundits, commentators and historians as well as their trainers and fighters. There are overlaps, of course, but neither the commentator nor historian is challenged as to how well they can fight. Their goal is objectivity and a bird's eye view of the activity of others as a whole. The goal of the fighter and trainer, though, is individual application – that is, personal victory. Through this process, this separation of labor, everyone benefits and it's the path Wing Chun should follow as well.

The name of Mike Tyson is synonymous with fistic skill, power, intimidation and speed. But it should be known that it was his trainer – Cus D'Amato, the venerable boxing historian and mad scientist/philosopher – that built Tyson. Cus was that rare breed – a man of ideas! He was a great boxing historian (something he passed along to young Tyson) as well as a unique thinker in terms of application that was also a personal trainer. Of course, Cus himself was not a world-champion fighter. Nevertheless, the products of his ideas did win titles (Jose Torres, Floyd Patterson and Tyson).

The great Wong Shun Leung was a man similar to D'Amato – both a deep thinker/philosopher and a trainer. Wong was interested in the truth. Period. And that was why his Wing Chun is still known and studied today. He was, in a way, Wing Chun's Cus D'Amato and Mike Tyson! But even still, the lesson must be that we don't rest upon

D'Amato's work, nor Wong's – or anyone else's. We must study the principles and keep pressing forward. Always forward with each new generation – not forgetting the past but also not being bound by it. The past should serve the future, not hinder it. To do otherwise is to give up living, to stop and hide in the cool shade of the history. When we do that, though, we lose ourselves and that thing we love.

After all, if one were to approach music as we do Wing Chun (in the traditionalist sense) music would be lost. If all guitarists were shown how to play only in order to play songs of old, and in a particular fashion like blues or rock but no other style, then new music would vanish. It's the same with Wing Chun. A musician will love his instrument, sure, but he knows it's a means to an end and he rightly loves the whole process. The instrument is the musician's servant for the greater goal of creating and/or playing beautiful music. Words and grammar are the writer's tools and he may certainly love them (I surely do!) but they are means to the end of communicating stories and ideas. The minute the instruments like guitars and words become ends rather than means, all music and literature are lost.

Wing Chun is no different.

NOTES

7. Philosophers of the Fist

1. The truth will, indeed, set us free. If all people are equal beings intrinsically - being created by God – then assaulting someone is a clear violation of natural order. But this violation is preceded by false ideas about the nature of reality, which leads invariably to bad character. The true martial artist must accept the pursuit of truth as their highest goal for this very reason as it's falsehood that leads to the very violence they train physically to repel. To ignore this mandate is like a fireman who plays with matches in bed at night.
2. Any practice of the arts of force that don't rest on the solid foundation of self-defense is inherently immoral. Sport fighting, when properly controlled by rules for safety, isn't necessarily immoral due to the fact that no one's free-will is violated. The action of violence isn't the issue, it's the trampling upon another's freedom that is the error. The principle at hand is that since God created all men, only God has absolute rights and freedom. For one person (or group) to use force to deny anyone their God-given right to free-will is evil because the aggressor is playing God.
3. Which is to say that there is an ultimate source of morality – God. This ultimate source must be God because He must be both ultimately authoritative and personal or else our reasoning breaks down. A polytheistic god – a one of many – has no ultimate authority and can't issue moral proclamations. If morality itself is ultimate as some kind of abstract force, we could never know it nor account for why physical matter (as a derivative reality) has any meaning. Thus, God must be both ultimate and personal.
4. Free-will and anarchy are not brothers. Proper use of authority – like parents lovingly raising and disciplining their children or schools having rules for students – are not violations of freedom. We must be careful not to confuse metaphysical liberty (God) with man's derivative political liberty. Free choices still entail proper authority structures like private schools, private businesses and individual contracts between consenting adults. These just (morally true, though derived and limited) authorities and free-will contracts absolutely must be honored. The breaking of one's word is an act of indirect force against the other party through fraud. We champion, therefore, a delegated liberty from the ultimate authority (God), not a "natural" or unique freedom, which would, of course, logically lead to anarchy.

12. Facing

1. Sure, he can try a spinning attack but these are far less likely and easier to repel.
2. Ip Man's most famous student, Wong Shun Leung, was encouraged by his Sifu to go out on the streets and test out his training. Wong, following this advice, and eager to learn whether or not his Wing Chun could work outside the classroom, took part in up to 100 semi-organized matches (beimo fights) with men from other kung-fu schools. These matches did have elements of restraint and organization but were critical in Wong developing a brand of Wing Chun that was quite combat effective. The culture at that time, unique in history, allowed for young men to engage in such fisticuffs for "skill comparisons". In a way, these matches were the centerpiece of Wong's training as they gave direction to his classroom work.

14. The Versatile YJKYM

1. In America, when you claim self-defense, the burden of proof has now shifted to you. What must you now prove? That any other reasonable person would have feared for their life and/or safety. To be flippant about this issue is to invite sure legal trouble, up to and including imprisonment.
2. Always be prepared to strike first should the situation call for it. The demands of morality do not preclude an attack that cuts off the enemy before they are able to launch first. Certainly, we must be completely certain of the rightness of our actions and be able to back them up legally.

15. Footwork...like Clockwork

1. A martial art technique isn't a question of morality, but of necessity and logic. The facing position is a principle, as previously described, that is inherently logical according to the demands of combat and the need of integrative technique and tactics. But these principles are not metaphysical principles, nor ethical commandments. Tweak them as needed but know that the more deviation from the norm the greater the risk of chaos and disintegration of your fighting system.

17. Contact & Infighting

1. Great boxing champions, you'll notice, have unique styles that fit their specific mix of physical attributes and temperament. Despite a sparse tool-box of technique, high-level boxers, not burdened by tradition as many in Wing Chun are, develop personal means of application. This should be the goal of the Wing Chun system too.

2. Ali can be said to have had two professional careers – pre and post exile. In his first career, where he was unbeaten, he was virtually untouchable – even when fighting blind as he was forced to for one round against Sonny Liston. The second career, after 1970, he was much more flat-footed and had to adjust his style accordingly. As great as he was, it's likely that we never saw him at his best. His peak years were spent giving speeches to college students instead of boxing.

18. Idolatry in Wing Chun

1. It's also important to point out that all people are religious in that they must ascribe ultimate authority to something. They simply must. If there is no ultimate then there's no knowledge or morality and everything collapses into *one-ism*. If one-ism (the pantheistic belief that all is one) is ultimately true then the very practice of self-defense is futile because there is no more value in one thing than another. Thus, life and death are of equal – that is, no – value. For self-defense to have any moral justification and/or value at all, the moral God of Scripture must be God. In this way, the question of ultimate philosophical/theological commitments are at the center of one's life and certainly the core of their self-defense.